Money and Inflation

Mehdi Chowdhury

Money and Inflation

A New Approach to Monetary Analysis for the 21st Century

palgrave
macmillan

Mehdi Chowdhury
Bournemouth University
Bournemouth, UK

ISBN 978-3-031-52355-7 ISBN 978-3-031-52356-4 (eBook)
https://doi.org/10.1007/978-3-031-52356-4

This Palgrave Macmillan imprint is published by the registered company Springer Nature Switzerland AG
The registered company address is: Gewerbestrasse 11, 6330 Cham, Switzerland

Paper in this product is recyclable.

Contents

List of Figures

CHAPTER 1

Introduction

Abstract The chapter starts with providing justifications for writing a new book on money and inflation despite the availability of many books, articles, and online materials. The chapter states that though those works have advanced the scholarship—they are insufficient in addressing money and money-related matters in the modern world. The proof is in the inability of nation states in managing monetary matters like inflation and the cost of living crisis. Moreover, those academic works are lacking in clarity as such general people, even trained academics are frequently seen to have no understanding of money. Accordingly, the chapter forwards the goal of developing a new scholarship on money and inflation. The latter part of the chapter discusses the writing style used in the book along with influences, and acknowledges the contribution made by various well-wishers.

Keywords Cost of living crisis · Debt crisis · Definition of money · Covid-19 · Central banks · Political turmoil

The introduction should start stating the purpose of writing a book on money and inflation. It is an obvious question as already so many books, articles, and blogs have been written on this subject matter. Consequently,

M. Chowdhury, *Money and Inflation*,
https://doi.org/10.1007/978-3-031-52356-4_1

it may appear that we already know everything about money and money-related matter like inflation, and a new book can hardly add any value to this extensive body of literature.

I object! The book starts with the premise that our knowledge of money is limited, so is our understanding of inflation. The proof is in the pudding—manifested in the increasing inability of nation states in controlling money-related matters of the twenty-first century. Monetary matters already resulted in ousting a number of governments in the last 2–3 years in various parts of the world. Many countries are now in serious debt and facing subsequent economic and political turmoil. The term inflation is now in headlines all around the globe. If we already know what money is and the subsequent causes of inflation, then why can we not do something about it, or at least communicate in an intelligible manner? Unfortunately, that is something not seen.

This demonstrates the need to rethink our understanding of money and money-related matters. It does not mean that the old knowledge is to be completely discarded, instead to realise that our existing understanding of money is incomplete; as well as inadequate to face contemporary challenges. Unless we attempt that journey to rethink *what is money* and the causes of inflation or the recent cost of living crisis; the relevant public policies on monetary matters will always fall short.

The claim of an incomplete knowledge sounds extraordinary given the availability of many books, articles, and commentaries analysing money and money-related matters. Still, most of those are lacking in a single line of statement defining or explaining money and when given may appear in a casual manner as if the question of definition or explanation is not that important! This then results in other limited explanations on related issues. One example of such is the widely known view that the banks' creation of loans creates money in the economy. But why is this the case? The loan becomes the same as the money, but no explanation for the equivalence is offered. Then, the literature gets muddled with complicated terms that makes it nearly impossible for general people even trained academics to understand what money is. For example, the academic literature and policy-oriented bodies would refer to monetary measures coined as M1, M2 and others, but no justification for using those measures to count money is offered. Money remains a thing shrouded in a mystery. These complications of describing monetary matters were raised by A. Mitchell Innes, who is known as one of the most influential theorists on the matter of money. He recognised the difficulties as can be seen by the paragraph,

> As I shall have frequent occasion to use these two words, it is necessary that the reader should familiarize himself with this conception which, though simple enough to the banker or financial expert, is apt to be confusing to the ordinary reader, owing, to the many derivative meanings which are associated with…. (Innes 1913; See also Wary 2004, Chapter 2)

This observation seems was echoed by *Joan Robinson*, who also included the trained academics,

> The plain man has always found the Theory of Money a bewildering subject, but at the present time many academic economists are as much bewildered by it as the plain man. (Robinson 1933)

After nearly a century, we still seem in the same place as a recent book titled *Where Does Money Come From* states,

> Few Economists have time to do this research first-hand and most individuals in the financial sector only have expertise in a small area of the system, meaning that there is a shortage of people who have a truly accurate and comprehensive understanding of modern banking and monetary system as a whole. (Ryan-Collins et al. 2012, p. 11)

The above three examples surely establish the claim that our knowledge of money and money-related matters have significant drawbacks and trained academics including economists are not free from that limitation. Interestingly, sometime this question is simply shrugged away! Such as,

> When asked the question "what is money?", it will be answered with full confidence by any man or women in the street………. Economists will show considerately less confidence if confronted with the same question……… instead of designating what money "is" economists describe what money "does", or more precisely what something must do in order for it to be called money. In broad terms three major functions of money can be distinguished: (1) money as a medium of exchange, (2) money as a medium of account, and (3) money as a store of value. (Heijdra 2009, p. 319)
>
> It will be asked in this connection if a book on the history of money should not begin with some definition of what money really is.

> .... The reader should proceed in these pages in the knowledge that money is nothing more or less than what he or she always thought it was—what is commonly offered or received for the purchase or sale of goods, services or other things. (Galbraith 1975, p. 5)

The book instead postulates that the identification, or the definition of money is of vital importance. It aims to identify money in a manner that can be communicated easily to the common people as well as academics and to address the question of money directly; instead of moving to other issues as if defining money itself is not a serious matter. The book therefore is challenging and significantly ambitious. Specifically, the book is not restating the already known wisdoms as the premise is the limitations of those. Though the book acknowledges and encompasses the previous wisdoms; what the book claims to be money is novel to a certain degree and at first may be difficult to comprehend. But soon it will become obvious and appeal to simple intuition.

The book originates from the need to rethink monetary matters influencing the countries and the people all over the world. Almost all countries are now plagued by inflation and high levels of national and personal debts. But there seems to be no solutions, no clear policy guidelines. *Milton Friedman* said that high inflation is always caused by an unduly rapid growth of money relative to the availability of goods (Friedman 1968, p. 18). This global inflation and the consequent cost of living crisis therefore are at least explained by the increase in the money. But *what is this money* that has increased in supply? The usual explanation provided in the textbooks follows the monetary aggregates of the Central banks utilised to measure money. If that is the case, why are economies struggling to address monetary matters? The book will argue that money is more than those official monetary aggregates, and those measures cover only a part of the money in an economy. The rest of the money in the economy remains unaccounted for contributing to the failure of policies. This will be clarified in the book in due course.

The first part of the book addresses the question of money. The second part of the book deals with the matter of inflation. Strangely, inflation is a much less studied issue. While many non-economists studied money; inflation remains rather at the disposal of the economics profession, and unfortunately within that only appearing to have the role of a sidekick. The main role always goes to various policies aimed at growth and employment, and inflation is rather regarded as a by-product of those policies. Inflation itself seems a question not worth to be pursued. The book takes the challenge to rethink and redefine inflation expounding its clear relationship with money and its central role in modern times.

Chapter 2 of the book provides a discussion of literature on money as such the readers become familiar with the basic concepts and the existing literature. The definitions of various terms are provided where they first appear, as deemed necessary. However, this section can be skipped by readers who are already familiar with the literature. Chapter 3 is the foundational chapter of the book. This chapter first develops the methodology and then develops the concept of money. Various related issues are then analysed and explored in the proceeding chapters. In the final chapters, the concept of money is applied to explain inflation. This process may look lengthy, however, it is extraordinarily short compared to most writings on this subject matter. One important feature of the book is the use of examples. The examples are often simple and mundane as I uphold the view that there is no need to look for complicated examples when simple examples are available.

The style of the book is what I like to describe as semi-academic. In the process of writing, I consulted many books, articles, and online posts. Many of them have been cited. However, the arguments developed are not essentially the outcome of previous academic literature. The book uses a common-sense-based deductive approach, and the arguments and views expressed in the book are outcomes of that process. Academic articles/ books are referred to sometimes to show that the views appeared in some manner before, and sometimes that literature helps to consolidate the views. The book also uses many examples from non-academic fields such as movies, novels, online blogs/platform, videos, etc. I do not discriminate between academic and non-academic writings; a rather important matter for me to consider is the information and usefulness of those within the act of writing irrespective of whether they have been published in an academic manner or not. This approach probably helps to make the book also readable, and most importantly relevant and applicable.

The writing of the book to me was a process of discovery. I started to conceive some primary ideas from late 2020 and commenced writing around July 2022. But it started to get challenged and expanded in every twist and turn. The book that specifically helped to start this journey was a book titled *Money: The Unauthorised Biography* written by *Felix Martin* (Martin 2013), but the most notable to be mentioned is the majestic history of debt titled *Debt: The First 5000 Years* by *David*

Graeber (Graeber 2014). The style of writing also has the influence of the writing style of *Sapiens: A Brief History of Humankind* by *Yoval Noah Harari* (Harari 2014), which mixed storytelling with serious writing. This style can be also observed in the works of *David Graeber*. A preliminary draft of the views expressed in the book is available as a Social Science Research Network (SSRN) paper (Chowdhury 2023), published in March 2023. Since then, my views of the subject matter have further expanded. The book therefore has a large similarity with the SSRN paper with some significant additions. In writing the book, the most important realisation for me is to find that money is a central and inseparable ingredient of human life. Unless we understand the money, we will not understand the working of an economy. Inflation may not be similarly inseparable, but nonetheless an eventuality of modern living. These views will gradually become clear to the readers as they progress with the book.

In movies, the main actors are regularly shown to have been supported by others. They cannot accomplish anything without the support of the others. This is also how I wrote this book. Many people helped me during writing the book through suggestions and references to books and articles. Abdullah Yusuf, Peter Howard Jones, Munirul Haque Nabin, Syed Nizar, Christopher Hartwell, and Ian Jones are among those to be specifically mentioned. I am thankful to my family, friends, and relatives for their support, and to all those who had to endure my awkward sudden conversation about writing a book on money and inflation. Finally, I am thankful to my department colleagues at Bournemouth University, who shared their views and comments enriching this endeavour.

The post-Covid inflation is one of the motivators of the book, but Covid-19 itself was one of the influencing factors of the book. The grim experience of Covid forced me to rethink many aspects of life—like many other people all over the world. The book certainly has been influenced by my personal and associated global challenges following the pandemic that induced many to ask big questions about *life*. What else can be a bigger question than the question of money and inflation in our contemporary world? The journey of asking and answering these questions needed some degree of courage and a leap of faith from my side. Though finally the book is only over 100 pages long, it covers many overlapping issues, connects many dots from diverse fields, and consequently demands close attention from the readers. Yet, the readers, I believe will find the book relatively easy to read and the main message will easily get communicated; compared to other works on monetary matters. They will also be part of my journey to develop this new approach to monetary analysis. *David Graeber* stated "*For a very long time, the intellectual consensus has been that we can no longer ask Great Questions. Interestingly, it's looking like we have no other choice*" (Graeber 2014, p. 19). My hope is that the readers will find that in this book!

References

Chowdhury, M. 2023. On Money and Inflation. *Social Science Research Network*. https://papers.ssrn.com/sol3/papers.cfm?abstract_id=4406437.

Friedman, M. 1968. *Dollars and Deficits: Inflation, Monetary Policy and the Balance of Payments*. Englewood Cliffs, New Jersey: Prentice-Hall. https://archive.org/details/dollarsdeficitsl00frie/page/n3/mode/2up. Accessed 9 Sep 2022.

Galbraith, J. 1975. *Money: Whence It Came, Where It Went*. Houghton Mifflin Company Boston. https://archive.org/details/moneywhenceitcam0000galb_i7z8/mode/2up?view=theater. Accessed 27 Oct 2022.

Graeber, D. 2014. *Debt: The First 5000 Years*. 2nd Revised Edition. London: Melville House Publishing.

Harari, Y. 2014. *Sapiens: A Brief History of Humankind*. London: Penguin Random House, Vintage.

Heijdra, B. 2009. *Foundations of Modern Macroeconomics*, 2nd Edition. Oxford: Oxford University Press.

Innes, A. Mitchell. 1913. What Is Money? *The Banking Law Journal* 377–408. https://www.newmoneyhub.com/www/money/mitchell-innes/what-is-money.html. Accessed 26 Aug 2022. Reprinted at Wary (2004).

Martin, F. 2013. *Money: The Unauthorised Biography*. London: The Bodley Head.

Robinson, J. 1933. The Theory of Money and the Analysis of Output. *The Review of Economic Studies* 1 (1): 22–26.

Ryan-Collins, J., T. Greenham, R. Werner, and A. Jackson. 2012. *Where Does Money Come From?* London: New Economics Foundation.

Wary, L. 2004. *Credit and State Theories of Money*. Cheltenham: Edward Elgar Publishing.

CHAPTER 2

Existing Literature: A Brief Tour

Abstract The chapter discusses the existing literature on money, specifically the commodity and credit theories of money are analysed as they encompass all existing theories. The commodity theory postulates that money originated as a medium of exchange to overcome the inconvenience of barter. This theory is lacking in historical evidence; however, it well explains many modern money including cryptocurrencies. The credit theory, instead, finds the origin of money in the debtors–creditors relationship. This theory is increasingly gaining the acceptance of modern monetary theorists, and well explains the money creation by commercial banks. The chapter points to the need to develop a new scholarship as these theories are inadequate in explaining money. The literature on inflation is not addressed in this chapter.

Keywords Commodity money · Credit money · Barter · Medium of exchange · Unit of account · Wergild · Cryptocurrency · Stone money

This chapter aims to provide a brief tour of the existing literature on money. This chapter can be skipped by the readers already familiar with the literature and terminologies, however, the chapter may also serve as a refresher. It is to be noted that the historical origin of money is one of the common questions addressed by books and articles. But this is not an

M. Chowdhury, *Money and Inflation*,
https://doi.org/10.1007/978-3-031-52356-4_2

essential question for us, as money defined by the book always existed and will always exist. Hence the book is not interested in addressing the question of the historical origin of money, and such history-focused literature review is not offered in this book.

On the other hand, we must also note that money in the form of dollars, pounds, gold coins, and other known means have origins and were invented at some particular juncture of human history. An extensive body of literature addressed those questions, and the readers may consult for example, Davies (2002), Ferguson (2008), Martin (2013), Dodd (2014), and Kuroda (2020) for a general understanding, but these books are usually very long. A short but useful essay is available via the Stanford Encyclopedia of Philosophy (Stanford 2023) that readers may consult for a quicker understanding. Another group of works also have a historical view on the origin of money, however, instead of providing real evidences, only use logical arguments to establish the existence of the historical origin.

In the literature of money, whether they resort to a historical analysis or not, two concepts are prominently featured—(1) *Commodity Theory of Money*, and (2) *Credit Theory of Money*. The two ideas generally cover the whole literature on this subject matter including the historical ones. Dodd (2014) discussed some additional ideas on the origin of money, however, those are very much connected to either commodity or credit theories. Below the ideas of these two theories are presented.

The Commodity Theory of Money

The commodity theory of money views money as a commodity. Examples of such are cowrie shells, salt, gold, etc. The commodity theory of money proposes that the money has been invented for the purpose of facilitating exchanges, specifically to overcome the inconvenience of barter between people. Hence money has been invited as a ***medium of exchange*** (see Mishkin 2009; Chapter 3; Heijdra, 2009, Chapter 11) to overcome the inconveniences of barter. With this aim, a commodity was coined as money sometime in the past, such as shells, iron, silver, gold, etc.—therefore, according to the commodity theory, before this invention, money did not exist. The origin of this idea is traced back to *Aristotle*, though *Adam Smith* is the most renowned modern proponent. The use of a money token for the purpose of an exchange is also mentioned by Plato (1973, p. 58) but Aristotle came up with the first complete theory of the emergence of money. For *Aristotle*, money arose to avoid the complexity of barter. *Aristotle*'s *Politics* stated, "*For the various necessaries of life are not easily carried about, and hence men agreed to employ in their dealings with each other something which was intrinsically useful and easily applicable to the purposes of life, for example, iron, silver, and the like. Of this the value was at first measured simply by size and weight, but in process of time they put a stamp upon it, to save the trouble of weighing and to mark the value*" (Aristotle 1908, p. 42). *Joseph Schumpeter* wrote that *Aristotle*'s theory of money prevailed substantially until the end of the nineteenth century and even beyond (Schumpeter 1987, p. 60; Meikle 1994). In a similar manner *Adam Smith* stated that the invention of money took place to avoid the inconvenience of barter. For example, traders like butchers, brewers, and bakers invented money by considering a commodity as the *medium of exchange* (Smith 1937, Chapter 4).

> The butcher has more meat in his shop than he himself can consume, and the brewer and the baker would each of them be willing to purchase a part of it. But they have nothing to offer in exchange, except the different productions of their respective trades, and the butcher is already provided with all the bread and beer which he has immediate occasion for. No exchange can, in this case, be made between them. (Smith 1937, Chapter 4)

In a similar fashion, *Carl Menger* (Menger 2009) associated the emergence of money with its purpose of serving as a medium of exchange. *Ludwig Von Mises* (Von Mises 1953) treated the origin of money also in its role as the medium of exchange. This view also was echoed by *Irving Fisher* (Fisher 1911) when stating that any commodity to be called "money" must be generally acceptable in exchange, and any commodity generally acceptable in exchange should be called money (p. 2). *John Kenneth Galbraith* also used the idea of general acceptability in defining money in a rather casual manner that we stated earlier (Chapter 1 of this book). Money and the owners of money in those analysis appeared as separate entities.

Apart from what we have stated above, there exist many other books and articles explaining the invention of the commodity money to act as a medium of exchange between people. But many objected to the idea that money originated to overcome the inconvenience of barter (see Davies 2002; Martin 2013; Dodd 2014) and it is reasonable to say that it has been comprehensively dismantled by Graeber (2014) while covering the history of debt of the last 5000 years. In Graeber's language "*The story of money for economists always begins with a fantasy world of barter. The problem is where to locate this fantasy in time and space..?*" (Graeber 2014, p. 23; See also Dodd, 2014, Chapter 1). Hence money may take the commodity form, but it is not the barter that initiated that historical process.

The proof is very simple. If money has been invented as a medium of exchange, then there must exist real evidence, as it is referring to real people and time, but such evidences are grossly missing. This has been comprehensively discussed by Graeber (2014, Chapter 2) but the essential idea is that with the same kinship group, people do not barter with each other—"*barter is what you do with those to whom you are not bound by ties of hospitality*" (p. 33). This observation has also been made in Kuroda (2020, p. 35) that "*... credit transactions were used frequently enough to render cash transactions rare. Indeed, the most important use of currency was for very small transactions between strangers*". Hence barter existed between people not related to each other, but the butcher, baker, and brewer of *Adam Smith* living in the same village are unlikely to decide together a commodity as money to perform the role of the medium of exchange. But for strangers or for one chance meeting barter may have taken place can be seen sometime in the *Illiad* of *Homer*. Or in current times, it is seen by the exchange of jerseys with the players of rival football teams. Actually, with reference to *Illiad* it can be stated that commodity money may have been invited to facilitate another function of money as the *unit of account* to measure the value of goods and services in transactions. We find several mentions of money as the unit of account in the *Iliad* of *Homer* such as the prize items of the sport event organised by *Achilles* would often be compared with *oxen*,

> Achilles displayed before the troops the prizes set for the third event, the gruelling wrestling-match. For the winner a large tripod made to stride a fire and worth a dozen of oxen, so the soldiers reckoned. For the loser he led a woman through their midst, worth four, they thought, and skilled at many crafts. (Homer 1997, p. 581)

It must be noted here that the oxen were not getting exchanged, rather only served the purpose of counting or comparison. This is also stated by Graeber (2014, Chapter 6) in relation to the *Tiv* community of *Nigeria*, who would use brass rods held by men as a form of currency, but never would be exchanged. *Graeber* suggested that in primitive times, people would have debt to each other, and they would be generally repaid, but in the time of disagreement, the need for counting would arise and some goods were used in those counting and became money in that sense (pp. 60–62). The original proponent of the view seems to be *Philip Grierson* who suggested that money came out of the tradition of *wergild* (Grierson 1978; Wary 2018).

One lasting influence of the commodity money is that its existence made it extremely difficult to perceive the abstract nature of money. As commodity money is visible, often in the analysis of money, the visual representation of money becomes the dominating feature. Even the great abstract thinkers struggle to be free of the influence of visual representation. Karl *Marx*'s capital regarded money as a commodity and considered how that embodies the social value of labour,

> … the bodily form of this commodity becomes the form of socially recognised universal equivalent. To be the universal equivalent becomes, by this social process, the specific function of the commodity thus excluded from the rest. Thus it becomes – money. (Marx 2013, p. 57)

Georg Simmel's concept of the quantification also suffers from the influence the commodification (Dodd 2014), though he in general shared many abstract ideas. Even *Milton Friedman* in a lecture on money repeatedly referred to the term *printing of money* (see Friedman 2016, from 20 minutes), while also stating that modern money is not really printed.

However, though it cannot explain the origin, money exists in the form of commodity and in many ways has visual representation. Gold, cowrie shells, etc., have been used in the past as money. In prisons, cigarettes have been used as money (Radford 1945). A striking example of commodity money in recent times is the virtual money known as *cryptocurrency*, for example, *Bitcoin* and *Ethereum*. They trade like any other commodities on online trading platforms. In some places they are traded for real commodities (e.g. to buy coffee) and treated similarly as dollars, pounds, etc. Therefore, the idea of the commodity money surely has contemporary relevance.

The Credit Theory of Money

The alternative view, and currently rather widely accepted, is to regard the money to be arising out of the relationship between the creditors and debtors. The view is increasingly getting more accepted and shared by many, and importance of the credit money in economic history is summarised by Graeber (2014, p. 40) simply by the following sentences "*In fact, our standard account of monetary history is preciously backwards. We did not begin with barter, discover money, and then eventually develop credit systems. It happened preciously the other way around. What we now call virtual money came first*".

Credit money is a difficult concept to explain though it is observed everywhere in our day-to-day life. This money arises due to a credit relationship, a promise to repay a grant a favour (product or service) to the holder of the token. A famous example is the stone money of Yap island, which attracted attention of many (Furness 1910; Martin 2013) including notable figures like *John Maynard Keynes* and *Milton Friedman* (Keynes 1915; Friedman 1991). This stone money does not need any actual exchange of the token. Rather only the ownership is required which arises from a previous occurrence of the exchange of the ownership. In the stone money of Yap, the token is visible, but for credit money it does not have to be the case, as only the promise to pay is required, which is transferable from even mouth to mouth. A. Mitchell Innes is regarded as the main proponent of the credit theory of money, who shared the idea through two articles in 1913 and 2014. However, *Henry Dunning Macleod* seems to be the earliest proponent (Wary 2004, p. 11). The credit theory of money states, in Inness' description, "*Shortly, the Credit Theory is this: that a sale and purchase is the exchange of a commodity for credit.............. that the value of credit or money does not depend on the value of any metal or metals, but on the right which the creditor acquires to 'payment,'...........................,and on the obligation of the debtor to 'pay' his debt......*" (Innes 1914; Wary 2004, p. 51–52).

The above description does not refer to any commodity form as it is not an essential condition, however, it may take that form of a document stating in some manner *I Owe You* (IOU). This view has received such an acceptance that the *Bank of England*'s description of money used the explanation offered by the credit theory where money gets manifested by an IOU. This IOU can be passed to a third party and so forth, causing the IOU, i.e. the money to circulate from one person to another. This is what we see often in real life. Nonetheless, it seems that still there are issues in digesting the argument against the barter. For instance, the *Bank of England* comes up with an inconsistent explanation that money today is a type of IOU, but for the past, the Bank goes back to the usual explanation of barter (see McLeay et al. 2014a, 2014b).

Credit theory provided the basis for *Keynes* to develop his theory of money (Keynes 1930). According to *Keynes*, a *money of account* comes to existence with debt, hence does not exist before the creation of that. The distinction between *money* and *money of account* comes from the fact that money of account is the *description* or *title* and the money is the *thing* which answers to the description (Keynes 1930, pp. 1–2).

Though credit theory is rather based on stronger historical foundation and the modern bank money is credit money, still it is not well featured in textbooks teaching economics. A substantial revision is regarded therefore for accommodation of the credit theory. An important concept related to credit theory is the *State Theory of Money* which explains money as a creature of legislative processes of state (Knapp 1924; Wary 2004, 2014). Keynes also supported this view that modern money is mainly charterist, i.e. created through legislation.

Dodd (2014) extensively covered some theories on the emergence of money. They include barter, tribute, quantification, mana, language, and violence. Those views are also connected with credit or commodity theories and can be considered as a part of the wider umbrella of both theories.

Concluding Remarks on the Literature

In this section a short analysis of the literature surrounding money has been provided. This book views that commodity, credit, and other associated theories may well explain the emergence of money in various forms such as dollars, pounds, gold coins, bitcoins, etc. However, money exists beyond those manifestations, hence those theories are not well enough to explain money. The necessary arguments on this matter will be developed in subsequent sections. Some further discussion on the literature will be provided in those sections.

The readers should also note that the literature review is completely devoid of any discussion of inflation. As the book progresses, it will be made clear that inflation is closely associated with money and therefore a thorough understanding of money is required before commencing the analysis of inflation. Hence the analysis on inflation will be presented later, and the next sections are completely dedicated to address the question of money.

References

Aristotle. 1908. *Aristotle's Politics*. Translated by Benjamin Jowett. Oxford: Clarendon Press. https://archive.org/details/aristotlespoliti00arisuoft/page/42/mode/2up?view=theater. Accessed 8 Feb 2023.

Davies, G. 2002. *History of Money: From Ancient Times to Present Day*. Cardiff: University of Wales Press.

Dodd, N. 2014. *The Social Life of Money*. New Jersey: Princeton University Press.

Ferguson, N. 2008. *The Ascent of Money: A Financial History of the World*. London: The Penguin Books.

Fisher, I. 1911. *The Purchasing Power of Money*. https://archive.org/details/in.ernet.dli.2015.264286/page/n527/mode/2up. Accessed 7 Jul 2023.

Friedman, M. 1991. *The Island of Stone Money*. Hoover Institution. https://miltonfriedman.hoover.org/internal/media/dispatcher/215061/full. Accessed 25 Nov 2022.

Friedman, M. 2016. *Milton Friedman Speaks: Money and Inflation (B1230)—Full Video*. Free to Choose Network. https://www.youtube.com/watch?v=B_nGEj8wIP0. Accessed 6 Jul 2023.

Furness, W. 1910. *The Island of Stone Money, Uap of the Carolines*. Philadelphia: J.B. Lippincott Company. https://archive.org/details/islandofstonemon009573mbp/page/n7/mode/2up. Accessed 8 Jan 2023.

Graeber, D. 2014. *Debt: The First 5000 Years*. 2nd Revised Edition. London: Melville House Publishing.

Grierson, P. 1978. The Origins of Money. *Research on Economic Anthropology* 1: 1–35.

Heijdra, B. 2009. *Foundations of Modern Macroeconomics*, 2nd Edition. Oxford, UK: Oxford University Press.

Homer. 1997. *The Iliad*. Translated by Robert Fagles. The Softback Preview. Bath. First Published in 1990 by Viking Penguin.

Innes, A. Mitchell. 1914. The Credit Theory of Money? *The Banking Law Journal* 31: 151–168. https://www.newmoneyhub.com/www/money/mitchell-innes/the-credit-theory-of-money.html. Accessed 26 Aug 2022. Reprinted at Wary (2004).

Keynes, J. 1915. The Island of Stone Money. *Economic Journal* 25 (98): 281–283.

Keynes, J. 1930. *A Treatise on Money*. London: Macmillan.

Knapp, G. 1924. *The State Theory of Money*. London: Macmillan.

Kuroda, A. 2020. *A Global History of Money*. London: Routledge.

Martin, F. 2013. *Money: The Unauthorised Biography*. London: The Bodley Head.
Marx, K. 2013. *Capital*. Ware, Hertfordshire: Wordsworth Editions.
McLeay, M., A. Radia, and R. Thomas. 2014a. Money in the Modern Economy: An Introduction. *Bank of England Quarterly Bulletin*, p. Q1. https://www.bankofengland.co.uk/quarterly-bulletin/2014/q1/money-in-the-modern-economy-an-introduction. Accessed 22 Aug 2022.
McLeay, M., A. Radia, and R. Thomas. 2014b. Money Creation in the Modern Economy. *Bank of England Quarterly Bulletin*, p. Q1. https://www.bankofengland.co.uk/-/media/boe/files/quarterly-bulletin/2014/money-creation-in-the-modern-economy.pdf. Accessed 22 Aug 2022.
Meikle, S. 1994. Aristotle on Money. *Phronesis* 39 (1): 26–44.
Menger, C. 2009. *On the Origins of Money*. Auburn, Alabama: Ludwig von Mises Institute.
Mishkin, F. 2009. *The Economics of Money, Banking and Financial Markets*, 9th Edition. Boston: Pearson.
Plato. 1973. *Republic*. Translated by Francis Cornford. London: Oxford University Press.
Radford, R. A. 1945. The Economic Organisation of a POW Camp. *Economica* 12(48): 189–201. Reprinted in Readings in Microeconomics. Published in 2006. Edited by Khalil F. and R. Salim. Dhaka: University Press Limited.
Schumpeter, J. A. 1987. *History of Economic Analysis*. London: Routledge.
Smith, A. 1937. *An Inquiry into the Nature and Causes of the Wealth of Nations*. New York: The Modern Library. https://archive.org/details/in.ernet.dli.2015.207956/page/n7/mode/2up
Stanford. 2023. Philosophy of Money and Finance. Stanford Encyclopedia of Philosophy. https://plato.stanford.edu/entries/money-finance/. Accessed 23 Oct 2023.
Von Mises, L. 1953. *The Theory of Money and Credit*. New Haven, Connecticut: Yale University Press.
Wary, L. 2004. *Credit and State Theories of Money*. Cheltenham: Edward Elgar Publishing.
Wary, L. 2014. From the State Theory of Money to Modern Money Theory: An Alternative to Economic Orthodoxy. Levy Economics Institute of Bard College, Working Papers Series.
Wary, L. 2018. *Modern Money Theory for Beginners*. Recorded Lecture, 26 April, 2018. St. Francis College YouTube Channel. https://www.youtube.com/watch?v=E5JTn7GS4oA. Accessed 20 Jun 2023.

CHAPTER 3

What Is Money?

Abstract The chapter develops the concept of money. First, the methodology is developed, and then several hypothetical transactions are analysed. The analysis reveals that money is best conceptualised as the ability of a person/party to obtain goods and services from another parson/party. This definition of money increases the scope for economic analysis, as things usually not regarded as money become identifiable as money. The ability or money is an integral part of the context under which it operates. The concept of potential money is also developed, which is identified as an ability that may not participate in a specific transaction in a time and place, but is capable of participating in another transaction, in another time and place.

Keywords Follow the thing · Socratic method · Transactions · Use of examples and counter examples · Money as the ability to obtain from others · Potential money · Store of value

Until now, we have used the term money without providing any definition. It has been used in a rather casual manner. This will change from this chapter as it dedicates to develop the concept of money which will also later be used to analyse inflation.

M. Chowdhury, *Money and Inflation*,
https://doi.org/10.1007/978-3-031-52356-4_3

Methodological Considerations

What method shall we use to identify money? The development of methods usually follows from the readings of books and articles. The book, however, has not followed one, actually, most books or articles on money do not duel much to discuss the definition of money. They take for granted that money is already present, which is for them synonymous to commodity or credit, and the aim is often to address various consequences of the existence of money.

There is nothing wrong to start with the premise that money is already existing, and it also is the premise of the book. It is simply a fact of our day-to-day activities that human beings use money to buy goods and services. It is rather unnecessary to spend time arguing about the existence of "something", whatever that is called, in transactions of goods and services. Then it is more useful to look at that "something" causing or facilitating transactions of goods and services between people and the book essentially uses this method to answer the question *what is money*. The previous authors have identified the presence of various mechanisms in the form of commodity or credit facilitating those transactions. However, why not broaden our umbrella? Instead of looking at just a group of transactions, why not cover all human transactions of goods and services? Do we not see that *some other things* are sometimes causing those transactions as such not explained by our usual understanding of commodity or credit money? As they facilitate transactions, aren't those *some other things* also money?

The basic approach of this book is to follow transactions. This approach of looking at transactions of goods and services has some similarity with the *follow the thing* approach advocated by some authors (Cook 2004; Christophers 2011; Hughes-McLure 2022). It is not that the approach followed in our book has adopted the methods of those articles. Rather those papers helped to consolidate the methodological view of the author. Specifically, Cook's pioneering paper on following *papaya* that followed trade, production, and consumption of papaya is an important influence. Papaya in that paper moved several hands from farms to consumers. We, however, are not following in that sense, instead looking at the event of the transaction of goods and services between parties. This is justified by the fact that surely money as we understand commonly as coins, notes, and credit is used for transaction of goods and services from one person to another. But the economy is also consisting of transactions that do not fall into those categories. The factors causing those transactions are also money or at least equivalent to money. By following those transactions the question of *what is money* therefore can be answered.

Are there any other methods to be regarded as more suitable? I doubt! Keynes (1930) and Simmel (2004) also focused on transactions, as in transactions the functionality of money is most apparent. However, money is known to have other functions such as the *unit of account* or the *store of value*, specially, the *unit of account* given its importance in the monetary history (see Chapter 2). The fact is that money as the unit of account also reveals itself in transactions as this function becomes only relevant when it comes to the matter of a transaction—such as someone must pay back a debt (see Graeber 2014), or, as we have seen in *The Iliad* that *Greek troops* performing a service for *Achilles* through participation and *Achilles* giving them the prizes (see Chapter 2). Similarly, money as the store of value is only important when it has the ability to take part in a transaction. Hence transaction is the key event to be looked at.

Methodologically, the article follows a structure that may seem similar to the dialectical approach, which is already a common knowledge due to the dialogues of *Socrates* by *Plato* (see e.g. Plato 2002; Denyer 2014; Grève 2015). This approach is basically looking to find some fundamental truths through dialogues between parties namely the *questioner* and *respondent*. This is also known as *Socratic method* which also has influence in the works of *Ludwig Wittgenstein*. The dialogue may start from some commonly accepted incidences, facts, assertion, or truisms and those are tested through questions or counter arguments. However, this approach very much depends on the mutual understanding of each other. The participants in conversation must agree with the meanings as such the partner of conversation, i.e. the interlocutor, needs to follow and agree. In case of misunderstanding, a more detailed explanation of the points is provided to the extent that the interlocutor comes to an agreement. The arguments or examples are only provided to the point as needed, as expressed in Wittgenstein's response to the question of child in relation to the gravity of the earth (Grève 2015).

Similarly, the book progresses with plenty of examples as such any claim made by the book is subject to scrutiny and refutable with a counter example. This approach has similarity with also the approach of *Philosophical Investigation* by *Ludwig Wittgenstein* (Wittgenstein 1958, thanks to one of my philosopher friends for bringing this to my attention). The way the book progresses is rather a standard approach for scientific investigation. The reliance on examples, which can be questioned and tested, is an important characteristic of this book, which makes it different from some other books. In giving examples the book maintains an objective goal-oriented approach as such the existence and nature of things in the world are regarded as independent of how those are perceived or thought about (Britannica 2023).

From this point of view, *what is money* is independent of what the past thinkers wrote about money and even what the book is proposing about it. This book is only elaborating some facts. Keeping this in mind we follow an investigative approach. Though the book has a final goal, i.e. to provide an explanation of the inflation or the cost of living crisis observed all over the world, we do not, however, exhibit any moral preference in picking examples. This also makes the book distinct. For example, *Milton Friedman* demonstrated moral obligations to fight for the free market and against the government controls. *David Graeber* on the other hand had a strong moral position to fight against the capitalistic controls. But the book has a neutral position and is happy to take arguments/views from any side as deemed appropriate. This is reflected in some examples picked up by the book.

The arguments of the book start from the position that from our experience we know that money is used in transactions of goods and services. The money is therefore revealing itself within those transactions. From the specifics of such examples, this book identifies the nature of money and then identifies the existence of those natures in other transactions, and proposes to define money using those natures. Hence for us money is what is used in or causes transactions even if not visible in usual money forms, e.g. coins, notes, bank money, dollars, pounds, etc.

The book arrives at some novel claims about money which seem to have not been made before. However, we cannot claim complete novelty. We do not break away from the usual definition that money is accepted in payments (see Mishkin 2009). Lerner discussing Knapp's *State Theory of Money* defined money as, *Money, ..., is what we use to pay for things* (Lerner 1947). In our book also money can be interpreted as something that is used to pay for things. Hart (2022, p. 254) shared the view of money as a memory which can take both personal and impersonal forms that link individuals to their communities. In a similar fashion the book looks at money in both personal and impersonal forms connecting various segments of the society. Simmel (2004, p. 186) had mentioned a theorist (name not used) who stated all money to be claims on exchangeable goods. Our book is aligned with this view. Graeber's (2014, Chapter 6) analysis of honour and degradation is also closely associated with the view shared in the book. Hence many may have discussed money in a similar manner shared in this book; however, they have stopped short of making the arguments of this book, and the novelty of the book is in taking that additional step. The book differs significantly also in providing clarity and clear statements on what should be regarded as money, that are verifiable and refutable and applicable such as in the matter of inflation. The statement on money is not placed in any obscure position of this book, rather clearly visible to the readers and has the dominant position. Importantly, we have managed to transcend from the influence of the representation of money in some forms, which previous works apparently have not managed. It allows us to make some vital claims about *what is money* that are not available in previous works. Actually, in reading some other works, I personally sometimes felt surprised that how come the previous authors could not arrive at the views expressed in this book!

One may argue that this method presupposes the existence of money before providing a general definition. While previous authors would in general focus on the emergence of money in particular historical settings, we propose that money, as we identify in the book, has always existed and will always be as long as the movement of goods and services from person to person will take place. Money exists irrespective of how it is *defined*, hence we repeatedly also used the word *identification*. We already know that money exists in some forms such as bank money, coins, or papers as we all have such experiences. The societies already have the experience of something called money, which becomes apparent during transactions of goods and services. Then following the transactions, the existence of other forms of money can be proved. Cook mentioned about papaya,

> In the "wild", or in people's back yards, papayas are far from uniform. They can be monsters. Ten pounders! There are male, female and hermaphrodite trees (big herbs, really). (Cook 2004)

Accordingly, papayas can vary a lot, but there must be something common that allows the identification of those as papayas, for example, the taste of papaya. Similarly for money, the transaction of goods and services is the key. Paper money, coins, bank money, or cards all serve the primary purpose of facilitating the movement goods and services from person to person. Anything serving the same purpose therefore is possibly money and that is what we would like to identify. All of those, along with commonly known money like dollars, pounds, gold coins, bitcoins, etc., are chasing goods and services and contributing to inflation or the cost of living crisis. Unless all those are taken into consideration, any study of money and relevant policies or opinions will remain incomplete.

Finding Money Through Some Hypothetical Transactions

This section forwards some examples of hypothetical transactions. Though they are hypothetical, real-world scenarios have been mimicked in those examples. They, in essence, are evaluating the reasons of transactions between parties. In that, the general truth regarding a transaction is revealed. The readers of the book are treated as the interlocutors, with whom a conversation of the writer is taking place. The writer aims to provide explanation and examples enabling readers to progress with the book. This subsection starts with a simple case to identify a baseline truth, and then find the same in more complex examples. It will be shown that the fact observed in the simple example is present in complex examples. What can be identified as money is gradually revealed through these examples.

Case 1:

Person A	*Person B*
1 British pound	1 British pound

This first example is the simplest case and to some extent a trivial one as it involves exchange of 1 British pound for 1 British pound. As shown in the table, the case has two persons ***A*** and ***B***. ***A*** gives ***B*** one pound and ***B*** gives ***A*** one pound. The example illustrates a trivial transaction, but it contains the fundamental truth underlying the movement of goods and services between two parties. Assuming no transaction cost, the two parties would agree to have this transaction as it implies no change in the monetary endowment. Even if it looks pointless, ***A*** and ***B*** may agree to have this transaction. Therefore, we can make the statement that "*One British Pound has the ability to obtain one British Pound*". This statement forms the basis of identifying money in this book, as the ***ability to obtain*** is the fundamental condition of the movement of goods and services from one party to another.

The above transactional case is trivial, but interestingly many are likely to have experienced it in real life as the exchange of the one-pound coin is regularly observed in supermarkets. One-pound coins are needed in many supermarkets to release trolleys from parks. The use of coins also encourages shoppers to return trolleys to designated trolley parking areas. In supermarkets, often two shoppers will come face to face where one wants to slot in the coin to release the trolley from the parking bay, and the other one to slot in the trolley to release the coin from the trolley. They will time to time exchange the coin and trolley to avoid the trouble and time of slotting in and out. This is essentially an exchange of one-pound coins between two people, which many have already experienced.

It must be noted that we have used the term ***ability to obtain***. Instead ***ability to purchase*** could be used. It is also possible to state that one British pound has the ***power to purchase*** one British pound. However, we have used a general term ***to obtain*** which is applicable in both market and non-market situations. The market-based defined in our book are the activities with the presence of the acts of buying and selling. All examples of this section are referring to market-based situations. Further discussion on this matter is available in Chapter 4, but it must be noted that the term purchase is not appropriate in a non-market situation as the acts of buying and selling do not take place. Our identification of money extends to non-market situation and accordingly, ***ability to obtain*** is a much more suitable expression.

Case 2:

Person A	*Person B*
1 British pound	2 British pounds

Consider Case 2—both are endowed with money in the traditional sense, but a transaction is unlikely. The British pound is indisputably one of the strongest currencies in the world. No one will object that one-pound or two-pound coins are money. However, just recognising that those coins are money does not serve the purpose of the transaction. Two pounds has the ability to obtain one pound, but one pound does not have the ability to obtain two pounds. The transaction does not take place when the *ability to obtain* is lacking.

Hence, knowing something as money in traditional sense such as coins, notes, or bank money is not fundamental for transactions to take place. The transactions are caused by the ability. The ability depends on the context, hence the particularities of the situation, that create the ability, need to be also taken into consideration.

In the following cases, we will further explore the context dependency. *Irving Fisher* (Fisher 1911) stated that money is something generally accepted as a means of payment, which has been echoed in Lerner (1947), Galbraith (1975), and in many other places. We will show this an incomplete description of how transactions take place. Essentially money is entirely context dependent, and one must look at the peculiarity of the context to understand what is accepted for payment, or more specifically, *what is money* in that context. The notion of the *general acceptance* is not validated by the reality.

Case 3:

Person A	*Person B*
2 US dollars	1 British pound

In the previous section, we have discussed that one pound does not have the ability to obtain two pounds. In Case 3 we look at a transaction between two US dollars and one pound. ***A*** has two US dollars and ***B*** has one British pound. Assume that the exchange rate establishes that one pound is equivalent to two dollars. So ***A*** and ***B*** may reach an agreement to transact. We can state that two dollars have the ability to obtain one pound and one pound has the ability to obtain two dollars. In a real-life situation, they can be real persons or banks. It is also possible that one is a money exchange and the other one is a person.

To show the alignment of this case with Case 2, assume that the exchange is taking place in an airport. It is commonly known that airports offer less than what is offered outside in exchange of foreign currencies. Hence if the exchange rate is 2 dollars for 1 pound outside of an airport, the same 2 dollar will fetch less than 1 pound inside of an airport. But a traveller has no choice but to accept the rate offered once inside an airport. It is similar to the case of accepting less than 2 pounds by exchanging 2 pounds (as in Case 2). However, it is the context making that unfavourable exchange rate acceptable and creating the *ability to obtain* of a lower offer.

From the cases illustrated above, a clear fundamental characteristic is emerging, that is, for transactions a party must have the *ability to obtain* the desired item from another party, and that ability is context dependent. The context is conditioned by many factors. For example, a traveller inside an airport may avoid the transaction by already carrying some foreign currencies. Even if not considered unfavourable, a party may simply not be willing to exchange. For example, a British tourist in the USA may want to exchange pounds with the nearest passer-by, but that passer-by may not be willing to exchange dollars for pounds. Hence even if the exchange rate establishes the equivalence, the pound may not have the *ability to obtain* dollars from the nearest passer-by in that specific context.

The analysis therefore reveals that it is more appropriate to focus on the ability to obtain goods and services from others instead of identifying whether the parties are endowed with money in the usual sense like dollars, pounds, etc. A transaction takes place fundamentally due to *the ability of a party to obtain goods and services from the other party*. Analysing transactions via usually known monetary units deliver a partial or incorrect understanding of the cause of transactions, i.e. the ability. In the next chapter, we will also see that many transactions take place without the existence of those known monetary units. Therefore, money is better identified or defined as *the ability to obtain goods and services from others*. This ability is a combination of the endowments as well as the context under which the actors operate. The endowment of the parties in the form of dollars, pounds, coins, bitcoins, etc., explain only a part of that ability. The readers should also note that *goods and services* is used here as an umbrella term that captures anything including usual money in the form of coins, notes, or electronic signals, etc. Note also that in this example the *ability to purchase* can be used, as it represents a market-based situation with the acts of buying and selling.

Case 4:

Person A	*Person B*
3 apples	1 British pound

In the previous cases, only usual known monetary units like dollars and pounds have been used. But our identification of money required inclusion of things not usually regarded as money. Case 4 elaborates this.

Assume that ***A*** is endowed with three apples and ***B*** with one pound. In a real-life scenario, ***A*** can be a supermarket selling three apples for one pound. If ***B*** is happy with this exchange rate, the pound and apples can change hands. As the case is similar to the previous cases, it is acceptable to make the statement that three apples have the ability to obtain one pound in a supermarket. Then the apples are also acting as money in this specific example.

I would provide further explanation for those who would object at this point. They need to note that Case 3 and Case 4 are similar, that I have just replaced 2 dollars with 3 apples. It is easily accepted when I stated that 2 dollars have the ability to obtain 1 pound and therefore is money. But in Case 4, the same exchange is performed by 3 apples. Then why is 3 apples not money? If 3 apples are not regarded as money, then we run into an unresolvable paradoxical situation and regarding both apples and pounds a money in this context resolves the paradox. However, not only that it completes the logical loop, it serves the important purpose of capturing all human activities with economic consequences. The traditional views of money on the other hand capture only a fraction of such; as only the pound is regarded as money and the apples are not. Hence a large fraction of economic activities remains unaccounted for.

The first important claim of the book is that we require to identify money as the ability to obtain goods and services from others, whatever form that takes. The second claim is that following the identification of money, both parties must be endowed with money in an exchange and receive something after the exchange. The exchange does not have to be equal in our usual sense and an extreme inequality renders a transaction as one sided, which will be elaborated further in Chapter 4.

Case 5:

Person A	*Person B*
2 US Dollars	3 Apples

In Case 5, we assume that person A is endowed with 2 US dollars in cash. Assume that the event is taking place in the UK and in a supermarket. So ***B*** is the seller of apples and will only accept the payment in pounds. Hence the US dollar has no ability of obtaining apples and is not equivalent to two dollars of Case 3. The US dollar is not identifiable as money in this context as devoid of the ***ability to obtain.***

Case 5 is an important one for us. Instead of dollars, to illustrate the case, we may use any other currencies such as Bangladeshi Taka, Japanese Yen, or Euro. This example shows the limitation of our conventional analysis of money. Even if we know that the US dollar is the strongest currency in the world, its ability to obtain goods and services is dependent on the environment within which it operates. Therefore, a currency or any monetary unit does not have an automatic transactional power or in other words they cannot be said to have general acceptability. They have the ability in some places, but cease to have that transactional power in some other places. For this reason, people would exchange their currencies when moving to a foreign country. The currency of a country ceases to be money, i.e. *loses the ability to obtain goods and services*, when moves to another country. However, nothing changes in terms of the commodity characteristic of the currency. For example, if someone takes a ten-pound note to Japan, nothing changes in terms of the shape or design of that note. What it loses is only the ability to obtain goods and services from the Japanese markets and thereby plays no role as money in possible price hikes or the economic activities in that country. However, the same ten-pound regains the ability once returns to the UK. Hence the essential nature of a money is the ability to obtain goods and services from another person and this fundamental should be utilised to illustrate money. To take the example further, assume that someone has one million Euros available at disposal, however, that Euros may not have any ability to purchase goods and services in a supermarket in India unless it is converted to Indian Rupee. Hence, one million Euros is a lot of money in the European context but is not playing any role in transactions in a supermarket in India and is not money.

The preceding analysis demonstrates there is a need to free ourselves from the traditional view of money expressed in monetary units like dollars, pounds, gold coins, bitcoins, etc., as they alone are not ensuring transactions. In addition, many real-life transactions, which are to be explored in the following chapter, take place independent of the influence of the traditional monetary units. All transactions (using monetary units or not) take place due to the ability of obtaining goods and services from others and that ability may present itself in many forms. Hence money identified as the ability to obtain goods and services is most suitable for explaining transactions. In a market-based situation, instead of ability, the notion of purchasing power can also be used.

Further it is to be noted that, what ability can be regarded as money is context dependent. For example, in a money exchange, an individual can exchange pounds for dollars, but not apples for dollars. However, in a supermarket in the UK, cash dollars cannot be exchanged for apples, but can be exchanged for pounds in foreign exchange booths. Hence the money, that is the ability to obtain goods and services is context dependent. The US dollar is not money in a supermarket in the UK and apples are not money in a money exchange. But both of them can become money in other situations. This leads us to the concept of *potential money*.

Potential Money

Since we are focusing on transactions, the potential to enter into a transaction must also be considered; otherwise the identification of money will remain incomplete. All such abilities remain as potential ability unless engaged in a transaction. The *potential money* is also context dependent money. Some abilities have no transactional power in some contexts, therefore they are not potential money in those contexts. Such as a US dollar note has no potential to become money in a supermarket in the UK as that is not accepted in transaction. However, when there exists a potential, that potential money functions as the *store of value*. A type of money may not enter or have no potential in one form of transaction, but still can retain the potential to enter another one. Following from our example of the transaction between one British pound and 3 apples, it is to be noted that the transaction can be performed by any combination of one-pound coin and three apples. The remaining coins and apples though not exchanging hands, have the potential to enter such a transaction, therefore they are also money. In a similar fashion, 2 US dollars may not have any transactional power in a supermarket in the UK, but the same US dollars have the ability to contribute to the import of apples to the UK from another country. Hence the US dollars though cannot be used in a supermarket, have the ability to obtain goods and services from another market, and store the value when not used.

Intuitively, therefore, money used in actual transactions and the money available for potential transactions both are important in determining the price level, i.e. the exchange rate of the goods and services. This is therefore also explaining price changes and inflation. Assume a limited supply of apples and many people are willing to buy apples with an exchange rate of three apples for one pound. The sellers may see it as an opportunity and may increase the price to 2 apples for one pound. It shows a drop of the ability of pound and an increase of the ability of apples. Many may not be willing to enter in that exchange, but the presence of them with the willingness to accept a different price, i.e. 3 apples = £1, allows the sellers to keep the price of apples at a higher level (2 apples = £1).

What is expressed above is similar to what is observed in biddings. In a bidding, only one person gets to obtain the designated item. But the bid value and the purchase price of the item are determined by the existence of other bidders. Though the highest bidder wins, the other bidders also have the potential to obtain the designated item and their existence drives the price up.

Concluding Remarks

This chapter is the most fundamental chapter of this book as it develops the concept of money. The method and explanations provided in the chapter are not extraordinary as readers will see some alignments with usual economics textbooks. However, the analysis makes three substantial strides. The first one is the identification of money as the ability to obtain goods and services from others. The second one is the identification of the existence of money for both parties in a transaction, whether they are using money in usually known form of coins, notes, dollars, pounds, bank cards, etc., or not. Without this, the logical loop of this chapter is not complete. But more importantly, this allows us to capture the activities of the whole economy, beyond what is captured through the usually known monetary transactions. It also opens up the opportunity to look at the balance of monetary power of the parties involved in transactions. In Chapter 4, we will see that the balance may be so unequal that a transaction becomes a one-sided transaction. Hence the book is directly addressing the power structure of a transaction, without even adopting a normative viewpoint. Thirdly, we developed the concept of potential money, i.e. the stored ability to obtain goods and services from others, which is crucial to understand the modern economic systems.

The readers may struggle at the beginning to accept the definition of money provided by the book, but the usefulness of the approach adopted will soon become apparent. The struggle may be due to the fact that we have become so used to the usual understanding of money that other explanations become challenging. Even the famous monetary theorists, to some extent, are to be blamed. It is well known that modern money like dollars, pounds, etc., are hardly printed, but still the term ***printing money*** is used to provide explanations. ***Milton Friedman*** in a talk repeatedly mentioned the term printing money while also stating that modern money is actually not printed (see Friedman 2016, from 20 minutes). These diluted explanations incorrectly educate people by appealing to only sensory and visual apparatus. In order to understand money, there is a need to transcend from the usual known things or belief, and to move beyond to a more intelligible world. The readers are encouraged to make that journey.

References

Britannica. 2023. Objectivism. *Encyclopedia Britannica*. https://www.britannica.com/topic/objectivism-philosophy. Accessed 26 Jun 2023.

Christophers, B. 2011. Follow the Thing: Money. *Environment and Planning D: Society and Space*. 29 (6): 1068–1084.

Cook, I. 2004. Follow the Thing: Papaya. *Antipode* 36 (4): 642–664.

Fisher, I. 1911. *The Purchasing Power of Money*. https://archive.org/details/in.ernet.dli.2015.264286/page/n527/mode/2up. Accessed 7 Jul 2023.

Friedman, M. 2016. *Milton Friedman Speaks: Money and Inflation (B1230)—Full Video*. Free to Choose Network. https://www.youtube.com/watch?v=B_nGEj8wIP0. Accessed 6 Jul 2023.

Graeber, D. 2014. *Debt: The First 5000 Years*. 2nd Revised Edition. London: Melville House Publishing.

Grève, S. 2015. The Importance of Understanding Each Other in Philosophy. *Philosophy* 90 (2): 213–239.

Hart, K. 2022. *Self in the World: Connecting Life's Extremes*. Oxford: Berghahn Books.

Hughes-McLure, S. 2022. Follow the Money. *Environment and Planning A: Economy and Space* 54 (7): 1299–1322.

Keynes, J. 1930. *A Treatise on Money*. London: Macmillan.

Lerner, A. 1947. Money as a Creature of the State. *American Economic Review* 37 (2): 312–317.

Mishkin, F. 2009. *The Economics of Money, Banking and Financial Markets*, 9th Edition. Boston: Pearson.

Plato. 2002. *Five Dialogues*. Translated by G. Grube and Revised by J. Cooper. Indianapolis: Hackett Publishing Company.

Simmel, G. 2004. *The Philosophy of Money*. Translated by Tom Bottomore and David Frisby from a first draft by Kaethe Mengelberg. London: Routledge.

Wittgenstein, L. 1958. *Philosophical Investigations*. Translated by G. Anscombe. Oxford: Basil Blackwell.

CHAPTER 4

The Origin of Money as the Ability to Obtain Goods and Services

Abstract The chapter provides examples of the origin of the ability, including historical ones. However, it also notes that though examples from the history are useful, the question of the origin of money is rather about the analysis of the context that provides someone the ability to obtain goods and services from others. In a given context, the ability arises due to a game-like situation, where the outcome of the action of someone depends on the action of others. The chapter analyses both market-based and non-market-based transactions, and identifies that the creation of the ability is finally down to the use of the human body and mind. In a market, the parties can negotiate to exchange the produce of their body and mind. In a non-market-based situation, a party, such as a dictator can use the body and mind of the followers to extract goods and services from the rest of the population. In a one-sided transaction, a party may receive nothing or a very negligible amount in return. But it is the context that makes the money, i.e. the ability possible, and that may disappear or come back in changing contexts.

Keywords Market · Game · Human body and mind · Human biology · State · Central banks · Constitutions · Slavery · Labour camp · Force · Power

M. Chowdhury, *Money and Inflation*,
https://doi.org/10.1007/978-3-031-52356-4_4

In Chapter 3 we have identified *money as the ability to obtain goods and services from others*. A follow up question therefore is identifying the origins or sources of that ability. This section is dedicated to share the views of the author on this matter. In Chapter 3, I used some hypothetical examples to identify money. This section utilises some real examples as well as some fictional examples from books and movies. These examples establish that the identification of money as an ability is not just some outcome of a logical exercise; instead it is well founded on real human experiences.

Before proceeding further, it needs to be clarified that when discussing the origins or sources of ability, we do not aim to provide a historical analysis, though such examples are relevant from time to time. The question of origin is not about whether the money has originated at a point of time during the human history. Rather it is the question of the origin of the ability to obtain goods and services from others in the context of a specific transaction. The ability to obtain goods and services originates from a game-like situation, where the outcome of the action of a participant depends on the actions of the other participants given the context. In the previous section, some examples have been provided for illustration. Such as the action of offering a ten-pound note to a supermarket in Japan may result in no transaction between parties. However, the same note has the ability to facilitate a transaction in a supermarket in the UK, hence producing an outcome. A transactional situation can be identified as a game in which the outcome of the action of a party is contingent upon the actions of other parties. The literature that studies such game situations is called *Game Theory*, which naturally influenced the book. This book does not aim to provide an analysis of the game theoretic literature; however, the readers are referred to Maschler et al. (2013) for an excellent comprehensive treatment.

When analysing the origin, we are not bound by limitations imposed by the history and the incompleteness of human knowledge, rather the investigation is about existence within a context created via the existence of parties and the rules of their operations. This is what I mean by origin, i.e. the context that makes the money possible in some specific time and place. The money, i.e. the ability must exist when the human beings are engaged in transacting goods and services with each other, otherwise transactions cannot take place. By investigating the characteristics of each transaction separately, the nature of money, i.e. ability in operation in that time and place can be identified. This is attempted in this section by proposing some examples.

For the purpose of this section, I will classify transactions into two types—(i) captured by market and (ii) not captured by market. A market situation is characterised by the presence of usual act of buying and selling involving money in usual sense of dollars, pounds, gold coins, bitcoins, etc. In a non-market situation, the usual act of buying and selling are not present. This distinction of market and non-market transactions will be useful, though from the analytical perspective of this book, does not exist. As money has been defined as the ability to obtain goods and services from others, all activities fall under the single umbrella of *an economy* or *a social system*. However, later in the analysis of inflation, it will be shown that the shortfall of policies may result from the failure to address both market and non-market issues simultaneously and to identify the influence they have on each other. Thus, this distinction serves a practical purpose. Before making the viewpoint of this book on this matter clearer, it is necessary to analyse the origin of money as the ability providing examples of both non-market and market cases. That analysis is attempted in the following two sections of this chapter. In the third or last section, the case of *one-sided transactions* is analysed.

Market-Based Transactions

Market-based transactions refer to transactions with the involvement of money in usual sense of dollars, pounds, coins, etc. A market system operates through measuring and counting as such a barter can also be regarded as a market-based transaction. Such market-based transactions are captured in the national accounting of an economy. As markets are consisting of offers and counteroffers, they can easily be characterised by auctions—consisting of bids and counter bids.

Let us start with the examples provided in Chapter 3. Assume a transaction taking place in a supermarket in the UK involving one pound and three apples. The supermarket has the ability to obtain one pound as the person has the desire to have 3 apples, endowed with 1 pound and satisfied with the exchange rate. Similarly, the person has the ability to obtain 3 apples as endowed with 1 pound. In addition, the supermarket has the desire to obtain 1 pound, endowed with 3 apples and satisfied with the exchange rate.

Hence the ability of obtaining something is an interplay of several factors and those factors may have separate origins. For example, the person is endowed with one pound, which may have been obtained via some salaried work. On the other hand, the supermarket has the apples which may have been obtained from farmers. In purchasing 3 apples from the supermarket, the person is actually purchasing more than just 3 apples as it includes the shipping and services related to sales, i.e. commonly known as the transaction cost. Without any doubt, we can identify existence of three ingredients. Firstly, the apples themselves produced via the use of the body and mind of the human beings or farmers. Secondly, the human body and mind involved in shipping. And thirdly, the body and mind involved in the sales of the product. Some machineries may also be involved, that have come into operation via the use of human body and mind. Hence the endowment of three apples by the supermarket has the origin in the ability of various human beings to use their bodies and minds in performing tasks. It is akin to the idea of the labour theory of value well featured in the writings of classical economists like *Adam Smith* and *David Ricardo* followed by *Karl Marx* (Gordon 1959).

However, the *ability* utilised in creation or in transaction do not alone determine the price. Both parties must agree on a price and the determination of the exchange rate may be best described as an auction situation. In an auction the parties bid (explicitly or implicitly) for buying and selling of products. The bid value of an auction, at which a product is purchased, is usually less than the intrinsic valuation of the bidder. For the seller the bid value is the opposite, that is higher than the intrinsic value. The difference is the surplus and both buyers and sellers strive to have higher surplus.

Therefore, the exchange rate at which the sale is agreed depends on the bargaining powers of both buyers and sellers, which are determined by many factors such as the extent of the desire, the availability of alternatives, etc. Contingent on the availability of 1 pound and 3 apples, the bargaining power of both determines the ability of someone to obtain 3 apples for one pound and vice versa. Absence of any of the determinants may render a party deprived of the ability. The existence of the institutional arrangement facilitating that transaction is also to be considered. Take for example that the supermarket has closed its till for the day. In that case the transaction cannot take place even if both the supermarket (i.e. staff) and the customer have the desire and are endowed with pounds and apples. Hence the apples and pounds cease to be money in that situation. But they remain as potential money as both parties can come back to resume the activities the next day.

We so far looked at only the origin of the apples. What about the origin of the 1 pound, such as the one-pound coin? The coin consists of two things. The first one is the content and the second one is the name of the currency. The characteristics presented via the term pound reflect a specific country relation. Without the existence of that country, that ability may not exist even if a person is endowed with the coin. Now, looking deeper into the origin of the endowment of one pound by person, we came up with several possibilities. Such as one pound may have been obtained by some salaried work of the past. Hence this is a result of an exchange of the human body and mind to perform some tasks for some other bodies. It can also be borrowed from future, such as a loan via a credit card, which is obtained via the promise to perform some tasks in the future. It can also come from some gifts, charity, or social support services. These other sources must have the origin in some people performing activities using their body and mind in exchange for pounds. Therefore, money in the hand of a person in the form of one pound has the origin in the activities of human body and mind.

As for the content of the coin, the metal endowment of the coin also has the origin in human body and mind as the metals are obtained through mining. In the past the metal endowment was of significant importance in the marketplace due to the use of valuable metals like gold and silver (see Kuroda 2020; Martin 2013). This no longer is the case, and the coins are mostly accepted for their face values determined by the country that minted those coins. It is also to be noted that the one pound can also have other forms such as two fifty pence coins, electronic signals in the form of bank/credit cards, etc., or in the form of paper notes in some countries.

To complete this conversation, two further issues to be considered. The first one is the creation of money by states and the second one is the creation of money by commercial banks. The states or closely linked bodies such as central banks have the ability to create money in the form of dollars, pounds, etc., commonly known as currencies. The states have the ability to create money in the form of currencies just by constitution. Additionally, what we mentioned about the transaction between a person and supermarket is equally applicable. That is the ability of the newly created money of the states to obtain goods and services depends on others, i.e. the actual money (ability) is context dependent. The creation of money without any basis, such as printing of cash is regarded as problematic and attributed to cause hyperinflations as experienced in Germany in 1920s and Zimbabwe in 2009. This has been also cited as the reason for the recent worldwide inflations (Coomer and Gstraunthaler 2011; Graham 2022).

However, what enables a government or aligned bodies like a central bank to undertake the creation of money with or without any basis? It is simply the foundation of the power of the state which allows a minority group to govern the whole country. This power of governance can be bestowed through a voting process or can be appropriated by a dictator by force. But it is the human body and mind that enables it; because the power of a state comes from the ability of its various constituents, who use their bodies and minds. Without them, a state is simply powerless and so is the money issued by the state.

It is also known that in the modern economies, money counted by usual monetary measures are created mostly by commercial banks. Actually about 97% of money in those forms are created by those banks (McLeay at el. 2014a, 2014b), and this may be explained by a system of trust. To make the point simpler, note that in the past people would keep their golds and silvers with goldsmiths for safekeeping. They would issue promissory notes which started to be used as means of payment. The goldsmiths also used a portion of the deposited metals coins for lending which was an early precursor of the *fractional reserve banking*. Hence the goldsmiths or pioneers of modern banking created money through a system of trust. The modern banks essentially have the same operation but instead of tokens or metals only issue electronic signals in the name of their clients (Ryan-Collins et al. 2012, Chapters 3–4). In the past, it was the trust that would allow people to accept the money issued by banks. The same is continuing at the present though the process is somewhat more complicated (see Ryan-Collins et al. 2012, Chapters 3–4). In summary, the money created by banks are new money when human minds decide to trust them as money. Accordingly, once they are handed over to the accounts of the clients, the clients gain the ability to obtain goods and services from other people which is subject to the process discussed earlier in the example of a person and a supermarket. Note that the money created by banks follows the names of their state-issued currencies, which makes the bank-issued money acceptable. Therefore, the bank-issued money can function as money due to the backing received from the monetary mechanism of the state.

It is to be noted here that the market and non-market forces are intertwined in this world of money, and truly inseparable. The ability of a state to create money becomes possible by constitutions, and that money enters the market for transactions. Hence market and non-market forces are closely linked to each other. It can also happen at the individual level. An example is that once the skill of someone becomes desirable to others, it creates the potential for more money for that individual. But the *desire to have the good* is rather a psychological state of mind, which interacts with the market forces. An interesting example is available from a story about a painting named *Tondo Doni* of *Michelangelo*, now on display at the *Uffizi Gallery, Florence*. It was painted to honour the marriage of *Agnolo Doni* and was sold to him for one hundred and forty silver coins. Michelangelo initially asked for only seventy coins. But Agnolo wanted to only pay forty. Michelangelo was unhappy with this negotiation and asked for one hundred coins. Agnolo then decided to pay seventy coins as asked previously by Michelangelo, but this time Michelangelo asked for one hundred forty. The painting was then purchased by Agnolo at that price (Uffizi 1987). This shows that Michelangelo's skill was highly desirable at that time as it is now. As it was desirable, with the creation of that painting, money in the form of ability to obtain goods and services was created, which in the example was the ability to obtain silver coins. Hence the painting is an example of a newly created money through the use of human body and mind. The painting is also transferable from hand to hand resulting in finally getting housed in *Uffizi*. But the painting is money because it is desired by others. If a good or service is no longer desired, the market for that also disappears, so is the ability to obtain goods and services from others using that good or service.

Non-Market-Based Transactions

The previous section illustrated the challenges we face in addressing non-market issues. As we do not identify money in conventional sense, the distinction between what can be a market and what is a non-market becomes really blur, however, a non-market situation may be identified by activities, in which the usual act of buying and selling do not take place and scope for mutual negotiation is not present/weak. Another way to look at non-markets is that they cannot be identified as auction-like situations. When looking at such non-market situations, transactions taking place in those can be roughly categorised into three types. First one is by the ability of an individual, second one is by the ability of a group, and the last one is by the ability of an institution, such as a government of a country or a state body like a central bank. Again, these three types are well connected to each other and can be difficult to see separately.

A state by its construction has the ability to obtain goods and services from its residents. For example, assume a government increased the tax rate, e.g. instead of paying 20% the residents must pay 30%. The individuals or institutions of the country must follow this directive; otherwise, they may face harm, which empowers the government to extract goods and services in the form of taxation. Even sometime countries or rather governments may have the ability to obtain services in a manner that results in physical harm including death. An example of this nature is conscriptions for war. One widely-known example of this is the conscription of the legendary boxer *Muhammad Ali* who refused to participate in the *Vietnam war* and as a consequence lost his title, was fined, and jailed in the *United States* (Brown 2018). Another similar example of the use of ability to extract goods and services is the *Siberian labour camps* known as *Gulag* where the political prisoners were exiled and forced to perform economic activities for the *Soviet Union* (Britannica 2023a). These were non-market situations as the traditional act of buying and selling were not present and no scope for negotiation was also given. Needless to restate that the origin of such ability is not any debtor–creditor relationship or any negotiable arrangements, rather the ability of a state to force its citizens via police, military, law, and the supporters of the policies. It is true the most modern states operate on the basis of some form of social contract where the rules and regulations come into force by majority voting. In this setting the ability of the state comes from the mandate given by the citizens which in turn develops rules and regulations to be followed by the citizens. But in autocratic states, the ability is obtained by the ruling class by force, instead of the mandate of the citizens.

Therefore, money as the ability is very well suitable to explain these types of non-market-based transactions. The *Gulag* example mentioned earlier is closely associated with the system of slavery. This brings us close to the demonstration of the ability of individuals in obtaining goods and services from others. Slavery is an economic system in which some people known as slaves must provide services to other people known as masters.

Slaves are bound to provide the services and are at the disposal of masters. There can be bonded slavery explained through the debtor–creditor relationship (see Graeber 2014). However, the slavery may be also the result of a war and one may become slave by force without any debtor–creditor relationship to initiate the process. The slavery system provides the master the ability to make the slave work, thereby to access goods and services. The same goods and services can be accessed by someone via market in exchange of money. Hence the ownership of a slave gives a master the ability and this ability is equivalent to money of an alternative system. Interestingly the equivalence between having slaves and having money was stated earlier. McNally (2020, p. 17) stated about a letter from *Roman* stateman *Cicero* which mentioned about looking at a large sum of money, but the letter was actually referring to enslaved humen. This provides an example of the equivalence between having money and having slaves, as both allow for obtaining goods and services.

One important clarification to be made is that ownership and the ability are not really synonymous. Ownership gives the master the right over the slave. It is a necessary condition, but is not sufficient to extract services from that person. For example, if the slave is injured or already has worked for 15 hours that day, the master is unlikely to be able to extract any further services no matter what measures are available at the master's disposal. The ability to extract services is gained once the slave recovers from the injury or regains the strength to work. The readers may object that the instance of slavery in our example is explained as a transaction between the slave and master. However, a form of transaction does take place as the slave has the ability to provide services to the master, which prevents the master from causing the harm (see Barzel 1977 for an interesting analysis of the Economics of slavery). Hence money in the form of ability is at the disposal of both parties and gets transacted. The slave provides the service, and the master does not cause any harm. Therefore, this ability is also context dependent and has similarities with having money in usual sense. Having the endowment of money like dollars, pounds, etc., does not imply automatic ability to obtain goods and services, so is the case with the ownership of a slave.

A group can also employ forces to obtain goods and services from others. A fictional demonstration of obtaining goods and services using force is available via the famous movie *Shichinin No Samurai* (in English *Seven Samurai* (see IMDb 2022, Link https://www.imdb.com/title/tt0047478/) directed by *Akira Kurowasa*. This story was about a

Japanese village in the sixteenth/seventeenth centuries, that recruited some samurai warriors for protection from a group of bandits. The bandits came annually to loot the crops produced by the village, hence through coercion, the bandits were able to transfer sustenance from villagers to them. In return the bandits did not cause any further harm. Another slightly comical example of the use of such coercion is available in the movie *Kungfu Hustle* (see IMDb 2022, Link https://www.imdb.com/title/tt0373074/?ref_=nv_sr_srsg_0). This story is about a vicious gang named *Axe Gang* fighting for dominance over a slum. This conflict for dominance starts with two rookie members of the gang going to the slum for a haircut. Instead of paying the money, they show the symbol of the *Axe Gang* drawn on their chest. The symbol hence was the money implying the ability of members of the gang to extract goods and services through coercion from others.

This example of the movies may seem out of place, but a deeper reality is attached to them, that is how the token or commodity money may have come into being. Graeber (2014, pp. 49–50) discussed the history of emergence of the commodity money.

> Say a king wishes to support a standing army of fifty thousand men. Under ancient or medieval conditions, feeding such an army was an enormous problem .... unless they were on the march, one would need to employ almost as many men and animals just to locate, acquire, and transport the necessary provision. On the other hand, if one simply hands out coins to the soldiers and then demands that every family in the kingdom is obliged to pay one of those coins back to you, one would, in a blow turn one's entire national economy into a vast machine for provisioning of soldiers, since now every family, in order to get their hands on the coins, must find some way to contribute to the general effort to provide soldiers with things they want. Markets are brought into existence as a side effect.

In other words, *Graeber* described that the commodity/token money, market, and taxation emerged simultaneously to provide for soldiers. This explains why these fictional depictions of coercion in movies are so easily accepted by viewers. Because most of us have experience or knowledge of the use of such forces in some manner.

A depiction of the emergence of paper money is available in a National Geographic TV series titled "Origins" which is available to be viewed via *Disney+* (Disney+ 2022). This depiction is largely fictional, however, points to the link between money in various forms with the underlying ability of the issuing authority. Specifically, it shows that the paper money may have emerged through coercion, and it can be just an extension of the original ability of a person or institution. As shown in the TV series, a merchant went to the court of *Kublai Khan* to sell some precious stones. He was in return given some paper money. He was hesitant to accept but realised that not accepting those would result in execution. The TV series showed that merchant came out of the court utterly frustrated. However, the truth is that the paper money issued by *Kublai Khan* had the ability to obtain goods and services from the people, as other merchants under the rule of *Kublai Khan* were bound to accept that money. Otherwise, they would also be executed by *Kublai Khan*. Though the TV series did not state explicitly, this depiction of the power of *Kublai Khan* may have been derived from the famous book *The Travels of Marco Polo*, which was written by *Rustichello da Pisa* in the thirteenth century from stories told by Venetian explorer *Marco Polo*. The travelogue mentioned many instances of the use of paper money and even provided description of how they were made,

> With regard to the money of Kambalu, the great khan may be called a perfect alchymist, for he makes it himself. He orders people to collect the bark of a certain tree, whose leaves are eaten by the worms that spin silk. The thin rind between the bark and the interior wood is taken, and from it cards are formed like those of paper, all black. He then causes them to be cut into pieces, and each is declared worth respectively half a livre, a whole one, a silver grosso of Venice, and so on to the value of ten bezants. All these cards are stamped with his seal, and so many are fabricated, that they would buy all the treasuries in the world. He makes all his payments in them, and circulates them through the kingdoms and provinces over which he holds dominion; and none dares to refuse them under pain of death All the nations under his sway receive and pay this money for their merchandise, gold, silver, precious stones, and whatever they transport, buy, or sell. (Murray 1844, p. 137)

Strangely, this very important evidence of the use of paper money has been missed by many well-known books on the history of money written by well-known economists. For example, by *Joseph Schumpeter* and *John Kenneth Galbraith*. It could be that what is stated by *Macro Polo* is providing evidence of a state-controlled market system that goes against the belief that market is independent of the state, which is still maintained by many economists. *Marco Polo* even provided evidence of the creation of market by state,

> Now let us tell of the officers and barons of the great khan, and how he rewarded those who fought with him in the battle against Nayan……he bestowed, according to their rank, tablets of gold or of silver, on all of which was written,—"By the might of the great God, and by the favour which he gave to our emperor: may that prince be blessed, and may all those who do not obey him die and be destroyed." Those who hold these documents enjoy certain privileges, with written instructions how they are to exercise their authority…………….. They can take, whenever they please, and lead from place to place, the troops and horses of any prince or king; and whoever dares to disobey in any thing their will and mandate, must die as a rebel to the sovereign. (Murray 1844, p. 114)

This description is striking similar to what stated by Graeber (2014) as discussed earlier. These officials of *Kublai Khan* could not just go to door to door as it was rather time consuming and impractical. Instead, it was the marketplace from where these officials could obtain the services. Functioning of the markets and maintaining peace therein were rather advantageous for these officials. These both would require strong arrangement for observing rules and regulations. Consequently, markets are rather the outcome of the existence of strong states or institutional arrangements. Martin (2013, Chapter 5) described something similar; when the Roman empire started disappearing from the third century AD, so was the use of coinage and credit money in those provinces, as there was no central authority or the vessels of that authority to benefit from trading operations of inhabitants. Interestingly also, *World Trade Organization (WTO)* operates using the same principles. WTO has binding rules and regulations to ensure predictable smooth functioning of global trade or in other words, export and import markets. Another example of an intervention is the land reform by *William the Conquer*, who granted the lands of England to a small number of people in exchange for their military services to the king (Britannica 2023b). Hence the paper money or any state-designed money, becomes money as it gains the ability to obtain goods and services as an extension of the power of the state or any other bodies. This ability does not come from the money unit itself rather from the context that creates that ability.

Other examples of the use of coercion can be found in activities followed by colonisation. The coloniser may demand tributes from the colonised, where the colonised have no power to object. The stone money of Yap, which is already well known to the researchers of money, was associated with such an incidence as stated by Furness (1910, pp. 99–100; See also Keynes 1915). The *Island of Yap* was under the rule of the German government, who wanted to make the natives of Yap to construct/repair roads. They coerced them into doing so using the threat to take over their stone money, known as *Fei*. Hence the German government's ability to cause harm allowed them to obtain that service, hence was money in that context. Interestingly, *Furness* also mentioned that the stone money had no use as money in Germany, which is aligned with what we stated earlier that money of country may not have any use in another country.

Not just force, the faith or fear for afterlife may render the ability to some parties. This is observed in the functioning of religious bodies. The use of indulgences by the Catholic church in Medieval Europe is one of the examples. It can be stated here that Martin Luther's preaching against the indulgences is known as an important event in European history (Wengert 2015).

Hence a state or a group may in certain contexts possess the money or the ability to extract goods and services. *What is money* in a specific context is an outcome of an economic and social process. A similar notion was put forward by Zelizer (1989) stating that money itself is dependent upon social processes. Dodd (2014, p. 28) in discussing Simmel's idea of money stated that Simmel also regarded the value of money intrinsically connected with socialisation. However, emphasising on society or moral and religious values may put forward the notion that the ability come into being due to only some social agreements or negotiations. This does not have to be the case as already has been illustrated by the examples of the power of the bandits or the colonisers.

These examples above have sufficiently shown that institutions or groups have the ability to obtain goods and services from others and the origin of that ability can be diverse but, in many cases, can be explained via an asymmetric power relation. The individuals similarly also can have the ability, however, there is more to this ability which takes it beyond a socially constructed process. At the individual or social level, there exists a biological underpinning, and money exists due to just that biological underpinning. Actually, a significant number of transactional activities are tied to the biological nature of human beings. The money exists even without the existence of social norms, mutual trusts, state powers, or the forcefulness of a group of bandits. The biological underpinnings have even formed the basis of human societies and created money in other forms. Money in this sense always existed and will always exist as the transaction of goods and services with each other is indispensable in human nature.

To make this point clearer, let us take the example of lions and tigers. Both are top predators but have completely different social structures. Tigers are known as solitary animals where social behaviour is confined to mating and raising their young. They usually roam alone within a huge area. On the other hand, lions have a very different social structure. They live and hunt in groups. The evolution has made these two big cats' social structures completely different (Discovery 2023).

Humans always live in societies. This is likely to be the outcome of an evolutionary process; and Chimpanzees, with whom we share 98 per cent of genes, are also social animals. Actually, most apes are known to be highly social. The social structures and membership in human societies may develop and evolve, but each member of a society starts the life in a pre-existing society founded on human biology (Choi 2017; AMNH 2023).

Human biological needs automatically cause transactions and thereby money. To illustrate the point, take the example of an extreme case, that is a mother's love for her child. Most will agree that this is biologically determined resulting in a mother taking care of her child; and as we defined in the book, a mother performing activities for her child is equivalent to money. To further establish this claim, we note that in many places, instead of a mother, the majority of the activities, including breastfeeding, may be performed by a hired nanny. The nanny performs the role in exchange of a salary. The service of the nanny is therefore the result of the salary, while the service of mother is due to the motherly love for the child. The result of both is the same as they both are providing goods and services to the child. The salary received by the nanny from parents/guardians and the existence of a motherly love are money for the child. Existence of either of them provides the child with the ability to obtain goods and services from someone else. Not only that both nanny and mother are capable of performing the same roles, such as when a baby needs changing, the mother and the nanny both are capable of doing the same. They may do it with the same level of care! One example of the equivalence of a nanny's care with that of a mother is available via the highly popular and celebrated *Baby's Day Out* movie (IMDb 2022, See https://www.imdb.com/title/tt0109190/).

The existence of a mother's love is providing the ability to the child to obtain goods and services from her. Those who still have a strong objection are referred to the literature around the topic called *Unpaid care and domestic work*. The essential idea of the literature is that some household works create value, but do not receive recognition and are not counted in the GDP of the economy. This idea of monetisation of domestic work is generally accepted (see e.g. Luxton 1997 for the literature). As the arguments are essentially the same, there should be no objection in identifying the existence of money in the transfer of services from a mother to a child. The child possesses money, i.e. the ability due to the existence of the motherly love. This money for the child gets recreated every time the mother regains the strength, for example, when ready to breastfeed. Because of the influence of the biological characteristics the mothers also obtain satisfaction from taking care of the child. Therefore, this money is biologically determined.

However, beyond the core mother and child relationship, human beings also form bonding with other human beings, as they are biologically social beings. The need for friendship is common in all apes, including Chimpanzees, that human beings may have inherited. Even *Robinson Crusoe* of *Daniel Defoe* craved for friendship. Robinson Crusoe, as in that novel, lived in a shipwrecked island alone for 28 years. He rescued a native (in his language savage) from a group of cannibal natives. This act of rescuing was due to his plan for returning to the mainland but also due to the longing for a company,

> ……. The Disappointments I had met in the Wreck, I had been on board of; and where I had been so near obtaining what I so earnestly long'd for, viz – Somebody to speak to, and to learn some Knowledge from of the Place where I was, and of the probable means of my deliverance; I say, I was agitated Wholly by these Thoughts. (Defoe 2007, p. 167)

Following the rescue of the native (savage), who was named as *Friday*, Robinson Crusoe and Friday enter into several mutually beneficial activities, including providing company and protection to each other. This behaviour of providing services to each other is observed in every society. The transactions of goods and services therefore prevail in every social structure and are founded in human biology. This makes money, i.e. the ability to obtain goods and services from each other universal, existence of which is concurrent with evolutionary emergence of human beings.

The above discussion probably points that money is mainly founded on non-market situations of which human biology is an important ingredient. The various representations of money like dollars, pounds, etc., are also founded on non-market issues. The market belongs to a wider umbrella of an economy or society, and what we regard as market is actually an extension of things regarded as non-market. Without those non-market issues such as motherly love, the market cannot exist, e.g. the market for nanny. Without non-market issues dominating and shaping human societies, money in the form of dollars, pounds, etc., cannot exist.

One-Sided Transactions

So far, we have not explicitly addressed one-sided transactions. However, many transactions can be considered one sided. Examples of causing harms such as sending the political prisoners to labour camps and some instances of slavery can be considered as one sided. An extreme example of this nature is the incidence of murder. The murdered receives death and it is rather ludicrous to assign anything positive to that. Though in some cases compensation may be received by the family of the deceased; the incidence of murder can be placed as an example of one-sided transaction where the gain, if any, is rather with the murderer. A biblical example of the act is the murder of *Abel* by *Cain*. In Islamic tradition, *Abel* is known as *Habil* and *Cain* is known as *Qabil*. This event is mentioned in both *Bible* and *Quran*.

The event of murder is, however, not without economic consequences. The consequences are felt by both parties, in negative or positive ways. Unfortunately, what we mentioned comparing between a mother, nanny and child is to some extent applicable, that there is something in the relationship between the murderer and the murdered that causes the event. This is what well-known detective stories would always try to investigate, though this heinous act is also possible without any previous connection.

Actually, what the incidence of murder shows is that the question of symmetry or equivalence is not the key to an exchange. In the exchange, one party may receive harm instead of what is regarded as gain. Surely it is true for the examples given in the previous section about the use of coercion to obtain goods and services from the other parties. This is also true in the master and slave relationship, when the slave is forced to work for the master. Such is the case in the *Gulag* labour camps as we mentioned before. Even the prisoners of the camp were allowed to live for the time being, it is unlikely that they considered the imprisonment as any form of gain. A very grime example is also available in the Novel *Candide* by *Voltaire*. In the novel, the main character came to know of an incidence of cannibalism by the starving soldiers during the siege of a city. The soldiers were about to eat a group of imprisoned women but finally decided to only take the meat from a buttock adhering to the sermon of a preacher. In Voltaire's language,

> We had with us a very devout imam, who in an eloquent sermon persuaded them not to kill us outright. 'Only cut off one of the buttocks from each of these ladies,' he said, 'and you will find an excellent meal. If you need more, you can in a few days have recourse to its fellow'. (Voltaire 2014, p. 99)

Voltaire used a mocking tone, but the extremity remains unhidden and no wonder that people who read the book at that time were severely shocked. What we see in this is an asymmetry in exchange. The ladies were allowed to live, but they had no say in the harm that was inflicted upon them. The source of the asymmetry is the asymmetry of power relationship between the parties. The ladies were captive and were at the mercy of the captors.

In the examples provided above, the asymmetric nature of the power relationship is clearly visible. But the clarity may not be there all the time. Sometimes it can even be forgotten. It is always there, when people are not provided with any choice, but when provided with choices, the asymmetry is still present in most, if not in all cases. Accordingly, some exchanges may be better described as one sided, where the parties with power may be able to extract a far greater amount from the other parties and the parties with negligible power may just except whatever is offered. Consequently, it may appear that the parties with power possess all the money, i.e. the ability to obtain goods and services from others.

However, there is a limit to this power, i.e. ability or money. No one can be murdered twice. Once someone is murdered, the ability to commit the act gets destroyed and so is the money including the potential ones attached in the relationship between the perpetrator and the victim. The ability never resides in the hand of one party. It is the existence of the other party that makes the money possible and in situations that look like one sided also has a conditional existence and faces the same limitations as discussed previously.

References

AMNH, 2023. *DNA: Comparing Humans and Chimps*. American Museum of Natural History. https://www.amnh.org/exhibitions/permanent/human-origins/understanding-our-past/dna-comparing-humans-and-chimps#:~:text=But%20for%20a%20clear%20understanding,98.8%20percent%20of%20their%20DNA. Accessed 25 Jun 2023.

Barzel, Y. 1977. An Economic Analysis of Slavery. *The Journal of Law and Economics* 20(1): 87–110. Reprinted in *Readings in Microeconomics*, Published in 2006. Edited by Khalil F. and R. Rashid. Dhaka: University Press Limited.

Britannica. 2023a. Gulag, Labour Camps, Soviet Union. *Encyclopedia Britannica*. https://www.britannica.com/place/Gulag. Accessed 24 Feb 2023.

Britannica. 2023b. The Normans (1066–1154). *Encyclopedia Britannica*. https://www.britannica.com/place/United-Kingdom/The-Normans-1066-1154. Accessed 26 Jun 2023.

Brown, D. 2018. Shoot them for What? How Muhammad Ali Won his Greatest Fight. *The Washington Post*. https://www.washingtonpost.com/news/retropolis/wp/2018/06/15/shoot-them-for-what-how-muhammad-ali-won-his-greatest-fight/. Accessed 26 Jun 2023.

Choi, C. 2017. Fossil Reveals What Last Common Ancestor of Humans and Apes Looked Like. *Scientific American*. https://www.scientificamerican.com/article/fossil-reveals-what-last-common-ancestor-of-humans-and-apes-looked-liked/. Accessed 25 Jun 2023.

Coomer, J., and T. Gstraunthaler. 2011. The Hyperinflation in Zimbabwe. *Quarterly Journal of Austrian Economics* 14 (3): 311–346.

Defoe, D. 2007. *Robinson Crusoe*. Oxford World's Classics: Oxford University Press, Oxford.

Discovery. 2023. Big Cats. *Discovery Network International*. https://www.discoveryuk.com/category/nature/big-cats/. Accessed 25 Jun 2023.

Disney+. 2022. *Origin of the Journey of Humankind*. https://www.disneyplus.com/en-gb/series/origins-the-journey-of-humankind/4tGBS4pdG6tD. Accessed 27 Oct 2022.

Dodd, N. 2014. *The Social Life of Money*. New Jersey: Princeton University Press.

Furness, W. 1910. *The Island of Stone Money, Uap of the Carolines*. JB Lippincott Company. https://archive.org/details/islandofstonemon009573mbp/page/n7/mode/2up. Accessed 8 Jan 2023.

Gordon, D. 1959. What Was the Labour Theory of Value? *American Economic Review* 49 (2): 462–472.

Graeber, D. 2014. *Debt: The First 5000 Years*. 2nd Revised Edition. London: Melville House Publishing.

Graham, A. 2022. Central Banks Drove Inflation by Printing Money, Says Former Bank Boss King. Independent. https://www.independent.co.uk/business/central-banks-drove-inflation-by-printing-money-says-former-bank-boss-king-b2083627.html. Accessed 27 Jun 2023.

IMDb. 2022. *Internet Movie Database*. Names and links of cited movies are in the article. https://www.imdb.com/. Date accessed, various date July–October 2022.

Keynes, J. 1915. The Island of Stone Money. *Economic Journal* 25 (98): 281–283.

Kuroda, A. 2020. *A Global History of Money*. London: Routledge.

Luxton, M. 1997. The UN, Women, and Household Labour: Measuring and Valuing Unpaid Work. *Women's Studies International Forum* 20 (3): 431–439.

Martin, F. 2013. *Money: The Unauthorised Biography*. London: The Bodley Head.

Maschler, M., E. Solan, and S. Zamir. 2013. *Game Theory*. Cambridge: Cambridge University Press.

McLeay, M., A. Radia, and R. Thomas. 2014a. Money in the Modern Economy: An Introduction. *Bank of England Quarterly Bulletin*, p. Q1. https://www.bankofengland.co.uk/quarterly-bulletin/2014/q1/money-in-the-modern-economy-an-introduction. Accessed 22 Aug 2022.

McLeay, M., A. Radia, and R. Thomas. 2014b. Money Creation in the Modern Economy. *Bank of England Quarterly Bulletin*, p. Q1. https://www.bankofengland.co.uk/-/media/boe/files/quarterly-bulletin/2014/money-creation-in-the-modern-economy.pdf. Accessed 22 Aug 2022.

McNally, D. 2020. *Blood and Money: War, Slavery, Finance, and Empire*. Chicago: Haymarket Books.

Murray, H. 1844. *The Travels of Macro Polo*. Edinburgh: Oliver and Boyd.

Ryan-Collins, J., T. Greenham, R. Werner, and A. Jackson. 2012. *Where Does Money Come From?* London: New Economics Foundation.

Uffizi. 1987. *The Uffizi: All the Gallery Room by Room*. Florence: Editrice.

Voltaire. 2014. *Candide and Other Works*. Translated by Fowler James. Ware: Wordsworth Editions.

Wengert, T.J. 2015. Martin Luther's Preaching an Indulgence in January 1517. *Lutheran Quarterly* 29: 62–75.

Zelizer, V. 1989. The Social Meaning of Money: "Special Monies." *American Journal of Sociology* 95 (2): 342–377.

CHAPTER 5

Money as the Ability Vis-à-Vis Other Concepts

Abstract The chapter analyses the relationship between money as the ability and the other theories, namely the commodity and credit theories of money. The chapter demonstrates that money identified as the ability to obtain goods and services from others encompasses both theories, and it also explains transactions not explained by any of these theories. The chapter sheds some light on the process of development of modern commodity money. However, a commodity money is only money due to the existence of some other mechanisms allowing that commodity holders to have the ability to obtain goods and services from others. Similarly, a credit money is money as it allows the holders to obtain goods and services from other people. The chapter provides several examples of money that can be explained neither by commodity or credit theories.

Keywords Human origin · Origin of written language · Cryptocurrency · Labour camps · Human biology · Debt

The analysis of the previous section provided us with a comprehensive understanding of money; that is the ability to obtain goods as services from others should be regarded as money irrespective of the form taken by that ability. Where the act of buying and selling takes place, money can be also viewed as purchasing power, but ability to obtain remains a

M. Chowdhury, *Money and Inflation*,
https://doi.org/10.1007/978-3-031-52356-4_5

superior concept. This chapter evaluates the link between other theories of money and shows that the concept of the ***ability to obtain*** encompassed all those understandings. The discussion of this chapter focuses on the commodity and credit theories as they more or less encompass all other views on money. The chapter provides an analysis of the inability of commodity theory and credit theory in explaining transactions including some historical ones. It demonstrates that money identified as the ability accommodates both commodity money and credit money as well as money in other forms and thereby is widely applicable.

Commodity Money

The commodity theory of money views money as a commodity. Examples of such are cowrie shells, salt, gold, etc. This view is not itself problematic as indeed money in the form of commodity is well observed all over the world and was the dominant form of state-based money until the recent century. The bitcoin type cryptocurrencies are also commodity money, though virtual.

The commodity theory explains the origin of money using the concept of barter, but the barter theory suffers from a significant logical loophole. In order to have a barter-based origin, there has to be some form of mutual agreement between parties to use a commodity or token in transactions. It is even very difficult in modern times, when the frequency of meetings is much higher. Then how is it possible in the ancient world, when the frequency of meeting was much lower, that two people would decide to have a common commodity? On top of that it is lacking in historical and anthropological evidences (see Graeber 2014). However, even if there is no evidence in the ancient history, it is possible to find evidence of money coming out of barter or something similar like mutual negotiation in recent times. Hence the challenge is two folds, (a) to explain the existence of modern money in commodity form arising out of barter relationship, and (b) to explain the modern commodity money from the concept of money as the ability to obtain goods and services.

To address the first challenge, note that there are several examples of mutual agreements or market-based solutions giving rise to monetary units in modern times. For example, in prisons, the prisoners were seen using cigarettes as money (Radford 1945). The Bristol money (Marshall and O'Neil 2018) was a well-known successful money that arose out of mutual agreement between various bodies including local businesses. The worldwide use of cryptocurrencies such as Bitcoin, Ethereum, etc., can be viewed as commodity money that developed through a mechanism of mutual acceptance or trust. These examples are therefore demonstrating the emergence of money via mutual negotiations. How is it then possible that commodity money did not arise during the ancient time in such a manner?

Our answer is that the emergence of modern money through mutual negotiation can be explained by the pre-existence of money in commodity or other forms. Surely money exists or existed in the form of commodity or dollars, pounds, etc., and human beings at some point in the history invented those. Take for example a newly independent state of modern times. One matter to come into consideration immediately is the establishment of a central bank and circulation of currencies. But central banking is a recent invention which originated in the seventeenth-century Europe (Bordo 2007) and newly independent states are now just following this invention by forming a central bank. An example of such is South Sudan, which is the latest independent country of the world. The country became independent on 5 July 2011 and quickly formed a central bank following an act of the parliament (World Bank 2023; Bank of South 2023).

Another interesting example comes from the origin of written language, which even could be linked to the invention of money in commodity or credit forms (see Dodd 2014, Chapter 1). Human beings now and in the past are speaking or have spoken thousands of languages for millions of years since the dawn of humanity, but only a small number of societies have managed to develop their own written languages. *Daniel Everett* in *How language Began* studied the case of the use of language by the *Homo Erectus* species that survived for about 1.5 million years before the arrival of *Homo Neanderthal* or *Homo Sapiens*. Homo Erectus fossil records have been found across a vast region starting from Kenya to China, demonstrating the propensity of the species to migrate from one place to another. It implies that they must have communicated in an organised manner. In his words,

> Homo species probably all talked about migrations. And their conversations about travel made the trip more enjoyable. Humans don't migrate like other mammals. We sapiens plan our trips, review them, celebrate and lament then. And erectus seems no different, from what we can tell from fossil record. (Everett 2018, p. 49)

Hence the *Genus Homo* managed to develop some form of language in early days. This development has another origin that many animals, even birds have mechanisms for communications, though not known to have a language form. As Everett puts "*Human language emerges from a much larger phenomenon of animal communication*" (Everett 2018, p. 9).

Though the human species has used languages since the dawn of humanity and or even before that in ape-like situations, the written language is rather a recent invention. Only a small number managed to develop a language in written form without an outside influence. On example of that also comes from Everett's another work with the *Pirahã* community in *Amazon* (see Everett 2010). *Pirahã* community has no written language, though has a highly developed spoken language. Interestingly they had no number counting system though had words recognising quantities like *few* or *many*.

Denise Schmandt-Besserat proposed that the written language may have the origin in counting. Her thesis looked at the development of the Mesopotamian cuneiform writing style (Schmandt-Besserat 1978). She demonstrated that the ancient *Mesopotamians* would use clay tablets (or clay tokens/balls) to keep records of transactions of items such as sheeps, grains, etc. They would first have pictures of those items on clays. These pictures later developed in the system of writing now known as *Cuneiform*. It was a very long process requiring contribution of many generations over one to two thousand years.

Though the invention of written language took more than 2 million years after the appearance of oral language, it is now commonplace to apply the method of writing to any other language. Sometimes, it is done by borrowing from other scripts (e.g. *English language* borrowed Roman alphabet) or sometime by inventing new alphabets using another system (e.g. *Japanese Hiragana* and *Katakana alphabets* were developed from Chinese scripts). People now even invent new languages and writing systems from nothing. They are known as constructed languages or *Colangs*. Probably the most known colang is *Klingon* language which first was used in the celebrated *Star Trek* series (see Luu 2016). This language even has a complete set of invented alphabets.

The *Klingon* language is probably the prime example of what we wanted to demonstrate through this discussion. It is that the origin of something happening at present is not necessarily the same for another thing that happened in the past. The *Klingon* language surely has been invented through some process of mutual negotiation/discussion and essentially to address the need to have a language for aliens. However, the ancient *Mesopotamian* language may have developed due to the incidence of recoding transactions on clay tokens. In a similar fashion, some modern money may have been developed to address the need of various parties and originated via mutual negotiation, however, it does not imply that past money emerged in that manner.

Therefore, some present money has originated to overcome the convenience of barter and/or by mutual negotiation, but this only happened due to the pre-existence of various forms of money. However, the modern money that are arising out of barter and/or mutual negotiations can be well expressed as the ability to obtain goods and services as any other previous commodity money. It is seen specifically in cryptocurrencies like Bitcoin, Ethereum, that are essentially virtual commodity money. They are only available as electronic signals but treated also as assets. They trade like any other commodities on online trading platforms. In some places they are traded for real commodities (e.g. to buy coffee) and treated similarly as tradition money like dollars, pounds, etc. Having more cryptocurrencies in those markets demonstrates higher ability to purchase goods and services. However, in other markets they are not directly accepted and need to be converted to dollars, pounds, etc., to conduct transactions involving real commodities. This is similar to the case we discussed previously that money of a country ceases to be money (loses the ability) in another country and requires to be converted.

The proceeding discussion shows that money in any commodity form must also have the basic nature of being a money, i.e. the ability to obtain goods and services from others. Otherwise, that commodity ceases to perform any role in transactions. The idea of money as the ability to obtain goods and services encompasses the idea of commodity money. A commodity money is simply a representation of the ability to obtain goods and services from others. Once a commodity is regarded as money through some form of mutual negotiation or by force, that commodity acquires the ability to obtain goods and services from others. Hence if salt is regarded as money, the salt provides the owner the ability. If salt somehow is striped of the ability, it ceases to be money.

Credit Money

Money arising out of credit poses a much bigger challenge as historical evidences are pointing that money as metals, tokens, etc., may have emerged due to some pre-existing credit relationship (see Graeber 2014; Wary 2004; Chapter 2 of the book). Therefore, the challenge is to demonstrate the existence of money without any pre-existing debtors–creditors relationship. We, however, are able to show that credit money only explains a fraction of money (even if can be the largest fraction), that is resulting in the transaction of goods and services between parties. It implies that money cannot be explained only using debtors–creditors relationship, and thereby requiring an extended explanation, which money as the ability to obtain can offer. Additionally, all money arising out of the debtors–creditors relationship can well be explained as the ability to obtain.

The credit theory of money states that money arises from the relationship between debtors and creditors. Then there must be an exchange of such between them proceeding that relation. What if nothing like that has happened? Take, for example, someone has purchased a lottery ticket with £2 and won 1 million. The person is suddenly endowed with a substantial sum. But, this is not an equal exchange. The person now has more money just by luck. One may argue that the money won by the person comes from a system of money, in which most people have lost the money and a small number have gained. That system does not matter at the individual level. For an individual, either money has been lost or gained, and only that is what matters. Moreover, often we do not have the information of what happened in the system, to establish a clear-cut link between the money in the system and the money at hand. To take this example further, consider the occurrence of people finding treasures in their backyards. Those people suddenly have access to more money but no associated debt. At the individual level, they just have more money at their disposal. Surely, at the individual level the existence of money is not fully explained by the credit theory.

Note that money or the ability to obtain goods and services from others is entirely context dependent. Hence someone finding treasure at the backyard does not automatically guarantee the increase in money for that person. It is the context that makes the treasure equivalent to money. An interesting but to some extent grim and unfortunate example of is the trade of *Egyptian mummy* during the earlier period of the Western excavation. It is well known that the robbers for centuries looked for ancient Egyptian burials for gold, jewels, and other valuables. But in the 1800s, The Egyptian mummy became a traded item. They were lying in those burials for millenniums and were not treated as anything of value by the Egyptian people. But because of the interests of the Western explorer/visitors the mummies received the status of treasure, and vendors in open places would display mummies for sale. Many photos are available of that time and the readers may consult FSU (2019) for further information. Surely mummy became an object capable of attracting other goods and services due to the presence of explorers and visitors from the Europe. Hence the possession of a mummy became equivalent to the possession of money. However, this money had no debtors–creditors relationship attached. It just happened due to a changing context.

Hence at the individual level, the ability to access goods and services from others is not explained by creditor or debtor relationship only. Nor it is explained at the national level. The example of the *Siberian labour camps* known as *Gulag* and other similar examples discussed in the previous section demonstrated that. It is true that many may feel indebted to the states and willingly perform services. It does not mean that all individuals would perform such roles due to the feeling of indebtedness.

To initiate the money creation through the debtors–creditors relationship, there has to be an initial transaction to commence the process. That very first transaction is beyond the explanation of the credit theory. *Keynes* stated of the creation of the money of account (Keynes 1930), but what makes that account come into existence? There has to be a transaction of some nature causing that creation, which debtors–creditors relationship cannot explain. On the other hand money as the ability to obtain explains that perfectly. This is what we see in the relationship between *Robinson Crusoe* and *Friday*. Robinson Crusoe saved Friday due to the existence of some human emotions, e.g. loneliness, looking for support, willingness to go back home, etc. (See Chapter 4). Consequently, when Friday was saved, he became indebted to Robinson Crusoe; and the further activities following that may be explained within the framework of the debtors-creditors relationship as well as the concept of the ability to obtain. Note that according to our definition of money, it is Friday, who had the ability to obtain services from Robinson Crusoe during that first lifesaving event. It may be a bit puzzling as Friday was in a destitute situation then, and we normally do not characterise a destitute person by ability. However, in that specific context, due to the existence of a being called *Robinson Crusoe*, who was looking for companionship, *Friday* possessed such an ability which was even unknown to him. The ability existed in a potential form and got realised in that particular instance. Compare this with the victims of robbery. A robber usually picks up lonely victims, like in empty dark alleys. It is simply to reduce the likelihood that someone might come to rescue the targeted victim. Existence of that potential influences the selection of a target and actions of a robber.

We have already given plenty of examples to show also that the money issued by state is well explained by the *ability of obtain* framework, such as the paper money issued by *Kublai Khan* (See Chapter 4). Similarly, the act of issuing money by the coloniser in a colonised area is well explained by the power relationship. The existence of a legal framework is pointless as a ruler like *Kublai Khan* or the colonisers are themselves law makers and breakers. As we have already discussed, the German colonisers in Yap made a law by themselves to destroy the stone money to force the natives to repair roads. Hence the paper money or any state-designed money become money as it gains the ability to obtain goods and services as an extension of the power of the state or rulers. The state or any other body may develop certain rules, but the ability does not come from the money itself but rather is bestowed by the context. Modern states, by constitutions, are empowered to issue money through central banks. When the central banks issue money, they utilise a process that creates debt on one hand and money on the other. However, the process can only take place due to the empowerment of central banks by states.

It must be noted, that a significant number of modern transactions are done through mutual negotiation. The exchange of pounds and goods between buyers and sellers in a supermarket, what we have previously discussed, is one such example. The ownership of money gives the buyer the ability to obtain, contingent upon the availability of that goods or services. Such money in the modern world is well explained by the creation of debt by commercial banks (See Ryan-Collins et al. 2012; McLeay et al 2014a, 2014b) and therefore the credit theory is well applied. However, debt and money are synonymous in this theory, but the reason is not explained. On the other hand, the idea of ability can explain the relationship perfectly, that is through obtaining a loan from a bank, a debtor obtains the ability to obtain the predesignated goods and services. It follows that whenever banks are extending loans, they create debt, and this increased debt adds to the overall money available in the economy.

However, as we have given examples, debt is not essential for transactions to take place. They can happen through coercion, mutual negotiation, social contract, altruism, or just biologically. Those activities may result in usually known money like dollars, pounds, and others. However, still, many other transactions are taking place in the economy without the existence of those usual forms. All together is the money in the economy and money in the form of dollars, pounds, etc., are only a part of it. As human beings always transacted goods and services with each other, the money also has always existed. Therefore, money has a central role in human existence, not a side-lined actor appearing sometime during the history.

References

Bank of South Sudan. 2023. *The Bank of South Sudan*. Bank of South Sudan. https://boss.gov.ss/who-we-are/. Accessed 5 Jun 2023.

Bordo, M. 2007. *A Brief History of Central Banks*. Federal Reserve Bank of Cleveland. https://www.clevelandfed.org/en/publications/economic-commentary/2007/ec-20071201-a-brief-history-of-central-banks. Accessed 8 Aug 2023.

Dodd, N. 2014. *The Social Life of Money*. Princeton, New Jersey: Princeton University Press.

Everett, D. 2010. *Don't Sleep, There are Snakes: Life and Language in the Amazonian Jungle*. London: Profile Books.

Everett, D. 2018. *How Language Began: The Story of Humanity's Greatest Invention*. London: Profile Books.

FSU. 2019. *Exporting the Exotic: Mummy Brown*. Department of Art History, Florida State University. https://arthistory.fsu.edu/ottoman12/. Accessed 9 Aug 2023.

Graeber, D. 2014. *Debt: The First 5000 Years*. 2nd Revised Edition. London: Melville House Publishing.

Keynes, J. 1930. *A Treatise on Money*. London: Macmillan.

Luu, C. 2016. Why We Love to Learn Klingon: The Art of Constructed Languages. *Jstor Daily*. https://daily.jstor.org/why-we-love-klingon-art-of-constructed-languages/. Accessed 21 Sep 2023.

Marshall, A., and D.W. O'Neill. 2018. The Bristol Pound: A Tool for Localisation? *Ecological Economics* 146: 273–281.

McLeay, M., A. Radia, and R. Thomas, 2014a. Money in the Modern Economy: An Introduction. *Bank of England Quarterly Bulletin*, p. Q1. https://www.bankofengland.co.uk/quarterly-bulletin/2014/q1/money-in-the-modern-economy-an-introduction. Accessed 22 Aug 2022.

McLeay, M., A. Radia, and R. Thomas, 2014b. Money Creation in the Modern Economy. *Bank of England Quarterly Bulletin*, p. Q1. https://www.bankofengland.co.uk/-/media/boe/files/quarterly-bulletin/2014/money-creation-in-the-modern-economy.pdf. Accessed 22 Aug 2022.

Radford, R.A. 1945. The Economic Organisation of a POW Camp. *Economica* 12(48): 189–201. Reprinted in Readings in Microeconomics. Published in 2006. Edited by Khalil F. and R. Salim. Dhaka: University Press Limited.

Ryan-Collins, J., T. Greenham, R. Werner, and A. Jackson. 2012. *Where Does Money Come From?* London: New Economics Foundation.

Schmandt-Besserat, D. 1978. The Earliest Precursor of Writing. *Scientific American* 238 (6): 50–59.

Wary, L. 2004. *Credit and State Theories of Money*. Cheltenham: Edward Elgar Publishing.

World Bank. 2023. *The World Bank in South Sudan: Overview*. The World Bank. https://www.worldbank.org/en/country/southsudan/overview. Accessed 5 Jun 2023.

CHAPTER 6

Money as the Ability and Some Related Issues

Abstract The chapter addresses some relevant issues before progressing to analyse inflation. Firstly, the relationship between purchasing power and the ability to obtain is analysed. Purchasing power is useful in a situation characterised by the acts of buying and selling, i.e. in a market. However, ability is a superior concept and applicable to all human transactions. Secondly, the issue of money creation, destruction, and transfer is addressed. It has been noted that money in no form is always transferable. Money creation and destruction depend on the context and transferability of ability. Thirdly, the universality of money is discussed, and it is noted that money is universal as human beings have always and will always transact with each other. However, its form depends on social and individual idiosyncrasies. Lastly, it is noted that money has many names, and is called using different names in different contexts. But the names should not confuse us, as whatever is called, whatever form it takes—the ability to obtain goods and services from others is money.

Keywords Purchasing power · Remittances · Liquidity · Slavery · Social norms · Human biology · Public goods · Ancient Mega projects · Wealth · Capital

M. Chowdhury, *Money and Inflation*,
https://doi.org/10.1007/978-3-031-52356-4_6

The previous chapters have established the concept of money as the ability to obtain goods and services from others. The latter part of the book will establish the relationship between money and inflation. This chapter aims to address some related issues that in general will complete the analysis of money. Some of these issues have been addressed in previous chapters and this chapter provides further analysis and consolidates.

Money Vis-À-Vis the Purchasing Power

Instead of ability, the term *purchasing power* can be used when referring to the market-based transactions. This is very useful in addressing the nature of inflation in the modern economies. Interestingly, the term purchasing power appeared in some well-known writings:

> Money itself, namely that by delivery of which debt contracts and price contracts are discharged, and in the shape of which a store of general purchasing power is held, derives its character from its relationship to the money of account, since the debts and prices must first have been expressed in terms of the latter. (Keynes 1930, p. 1)
>
> The term "money" is ordinarily used in two quite different senses. We speak of a man having "money" in his pocket, and we also speak of him as "making money," even when he is not a counterfeiter. I shall use the term solely in the first sense......... Money in this sense consists of anything that serves the function of providing a temporary abode for general purchasing power. (Friedman 1968, pp. 195–96)
>
> Credit is the purchasing power so often mentioned in economic works as being one of the principal attributes of money. (Innes 1913; See also Wary 2004).

Money therefore shows purchasing power, but the above examples fall short of making this clear-cut statement. In addition, we are stating that *purchasing power is money* instead of investigating the *purchasing power of money*, which is a separate issue to be addressed, though connected to inflation. Ryan-Collins et al. (2012, p. 10) stated about defining money in this manner by pointing to the relationship between purchasing power and liquidity. However, no explicit analysis has been provided on how the liquidity implies purchasing power.

When transactions take place in an environment with regular buying and selling, the purchasing power changes hand. For example, the seller gives up goods, i.e. the right to use those goods gets transferred to the purchasers. The purchasers give up money in the form of dollars, pounds, etc. Hence money in those forms has the purchasing power to obtain those goods. Once the money gets transferred the seller has the additional purchasing power equivalent to the amount of money. To see it more, note that in the modern world many transactions take place using bank cards. Nobody cares about the existence of that money in a physical sense, or where the bank money actually is. They only know that they have the ability to access some certain amount of money via bank cards, i.e. credit or debit cards. Once some of it is used, the amount available drops. For example, assume an individual has access to £10,000. If that person uses £1000 in a transaction, only a further £9000 can be accessed. Then having less money is equivalent to having less purchasing power.

Consider another example. Many people now have the experience of remitting money from one country to another country. For example, assume that someone wants to remit money from the UK to Bangladesh. That person receives income in pounds but in Bangladesh the currency is Taka. Assume that the person wants to remit £500 and instructed the bank to remit that money to someone in Bangladesh. In Bangladesh that person does not receive £500 but an equivalent amount of Taka. Through inter-bank transfers and the intermediation of the central banks, this conversion is achieved. However, whatever is the process in between, the receiver does not receive pounds; so the pounds do not move from one place to another. Only the ownership of the pounds gets transferred. First from the remitter to the bank in the UK. Then through some process to a bank in Bangladesh. The bank keeps the ownership of the pounds and provides equivalent amount of Taka to the receiver. The result is the decrease of the purchasing power of the sender by £500 and the increase of the purchasing power of the receiver in Taka to an equivalent amount of £500.

It is well known in literature that the money in the economy consists of lending made by banks. As we discussed in the previous section, no clear explanation is provided as to why the lending made by banks should be a part of money in the economy. When viewed from the perspective of purchasing power, it becomes obvious that a bank's lending is actually money. By lending, banks create purchasing power for the clients. The client uses that to conduct predesignated activity such as buying properties. The loan is not immediately returned but with some lags. Hence by creating loans with delayed return, a bank increases the purchasing power of individuals taking the loan, as well as the money supply in the economy.

The above analysis shows the idea of money as purchasing power well explains the transaction of goods and services. However, the term purchasing power is more suitable for a market-based situation where the acts of buying and selling takes place. Money as the ability to obtain goods and services is a much stronger concept encompassing both market and non-market activities, that is all economic activities, and therefore has wider applicability.

Money Creation, Transfer, and Destruction

How to explain the creation of money, when money is defined as the ability to obtain goods and services from others? For example, creation of money by the government, such as literally the printing of money.

It should be already clear from the discussion of Chapter 4 that our explanation of money as the ability is fully consistent with this mode of creation of money. Assume a country with a certain currency, and the government has the power to print money and buy goods and services using that. Hence two acts are taking place essentially; one is printing cash and second is acquiring goods and services. By printing money, the government creates the ability to acquire goods and services from others. Therefore, money is getting created with such acts of the government.

For any party the money gets destroyed once that is used. But in return that party receives goods and services, which could be the money of the other party in transaction. That money may not remain money after the exchange. For example, assume someone purchased an apple from a supermarket. For the purchaser, if that apple has no more ability to acquire any goods and services by engaging in another transaction, it ceases to be a money. Another such example is obsolete or damaged notes; lacking the purchasing power though in past participated in transactions.

This brings us to the question of liquidity. In the market economy, money has some degree of mobility, i.e. can be used readily, which is synonymous to the concept of liquidity. For example, money in the cash form can transfer through several hands without any barriers. How about the other forms of money that this book refers to? Are they also mobile in a manner similar to cash or credit? Let us analyse it within the context of slavery, that we have used as an example.

The slave works for the master. As we discussed, the money of the master, in the form of the ability to extract a service, is destroyed once used. However, does that get transferred to the slave? The nature of relationship between the master and slave is that, if the service is not performed the master has the ability to harm the slave. Not only that, the master also has the ability to harm at any time. So, what the slave receives in return of the service is the ability to avoid that harm for some time period or the period when the task is performed. But like cash, credit, or cryptocurrencies in modern economy, can they be transferred to others?

The fact is that money in no form is always transferable. They are all context dependent. Such as pounds and dollars cease to be money when entering another territory, implying being stripped of the property of liquidity. This is more prominent for currencies of weaker economies. Moreover, money in the form of bank deposits such as fixed deposits is much less liquid. Sometimes, they cannot be used in transactions, rather at first need to be converted to current deposits and then can be used for transactions.

The same is applicable to money only available in the form of ability. Let us go back to the example of the slave and master. We previously discussed that the master is capable of causing harm to the slave so *not causing a harm* is what received by the slave in the transactions. Let us now evaluate what may be implied by *not causing a harm*. For example, it may imply that the slave is allowed to return to the family. So, not suffering from a harm allows the slave to enjoy the time with family members, which is a form of transfer of services within the family. Not causing a harm may mean that the slave family is provided with sustenance, which can be consumed and even transferred to others in exchange for goods and services. It is also possible to have some surplus (though seems unusual) in the slave–master relationship. Assume that a master may be capable of extracting 12 hours of service in exchange of *not causing the harm*, but only 10 hours of service have been extracted. In that case, the slave has 2 hours of surplus that can be considered as a form of gain, which in the context of our paper is a form of monetary gain as the slave has the ability to work for two more hours. However, if the slave works for 12 hours and is barely allowed to live only, nothing may remain as transferable. The master on the other hand obtains goods and services via the work of the slave. If the goods and services are not transferable implying has no ability to obtain further goods and services, those goods and services cease to be money. However, if those goods and services have the ability to enter another transaction with a third party, then act as money.

We have previously given the example (See Chapter 4) of the painting of *Michelangelo*. The painting was money, i.e. had the ability to extract goods and services as it was desired by others. As long as any such articles are desired by others, those remain as money. If an article is destroyed, it loses the ability to enter any further transaction hence cease to be money.

In Chapter 4, we discussed one-sided transaction. An extreme example of such is murder. Interestingly the murder may be capable of entering a series of transactions with the potential victim of murder. We have previously referred to the novel *Candide* by *Voltaire* where the preacher prevented the killing of the enslaved women from the starved army. He made it possible by the promise to please the heaven by stating "*Heaven will smile upon so charitable an action, and you will be relieved*" (Voltaire 2014, p. 99). Hence this serves as an extreme example where the murderer/killer is better off by not taking the extreme path and by the possibility of repeated interaction with the other party. But when the extreme event of a killing takes place, all other possibilities perish and the money on those possible transactions cease to exist.

This teaches that the money needs to be handled with caution, as usually advised, and the use of extreme measures may lead to the destruction of money. It is like to story of the *golden egg laying hen*, in which a farmer had a very special hen, that would lay a golden egg every day. But the farmer became greedy and killed the hen to get all the golden eggs from the belly at once. But after killing, the farmer could not find any. So, the greedy farmer eventually had lost it all. This story is also featured in *Aesop*'s fable where instead of hen, it is about a goose. But it is a well-known story all over the world, whatever the origin.

The killing of the hen in the story resulted in the destruction of all other possibilities. Surely the farmer managed to get the meat out of the hen but after that nothing more. This is often forgotten when people talk about the relationship between powerful and powerless, or rich and poor. The powerful may be able to extract more from the powerless—it serves the best interest of the powerful when extreme measures are not taken. Once that is taken, the power or the ability ceases to exist and essentially the money gets destroyed. Hence the manifestation of the power can be an illusion. This is also true when it comes to the wealth of the richest people of the world. In accounting terms, the wealth of some people may be over a billion, however, it does not mean that they have that purchasing power. In order to purchase goods and services from others, they will first need to sell their assets, which would significantly reduce the price of those assets. Furthermore, they will need to enter into transactions with other parties; and the success of that is dependent on the context and specifically the willingness of other parties. Therefore, the usual accounting of wealth overestimates the actual purchasing power. But this illusion or overestimation serves as a money as it allows the holder of the wealth to access desired goods and services from others. The continuation of the power is possible as they use only a small amount of money at a time. Never the whole amount of money as par the account can be used. Such actions will remove the illusion and the ability in that manner will cease to exist.

Universality of Money

The existence of money is universal, in the sense that it existed in all societies in the past, now existing and will exist in the future. This may seem like a self-fulfilling prophecy as identification of money in this book has been done following transactions, and human being always have transacted with each other in one way or another. But we specifically need to note that the types of the money, i.e. the ability to extract goods and services are context dependent and there is no universal form or representation of money. Though human beings have and will transact with each other due to the existence of money; the money causing those transactions differs and will defer depending on the social, and individual idiosyncrasies.

Before going further, a source of possible confusion needs to be resolved. On one hand we are stating the money is universal, however, also mentioning that there is no universal form or representation. This may seem contradictory, but easily resolvable. Take, for example, the word "I" which referred to a self or human being. Though all human beings would refer themselves as "I" or in equivalent words in their own languages, all Is they refer to are different. The word "I" referring to the existence of an entity but not the character of the entity as such the shape, race, history, or any other internal/external observable/unobservable features. The same is the case with the word "money". It refers to an existence and in this case the *ability to obtain goods and services from others*. But the characteristics differ depending on the social and individual idiosyncrasies, i.e. the context.

Now as the confusion or apparent contradiction has been resolved, we can move forward in demonstrating that there is no universal form of money. For this, let us go back to our example of a mother's love for her child. Most will agree that this is biologically determined resulting in a mother taking care of her child. However, activities that a mother would perform are context dependent. We have already established that the motherly love is a type of money for the child as it allows the transfer of goods and service from mother to child. It is true that a child receives services from a mother but what and how much, i.e. the provision of services by the mother/or the family is contingent upon the makeup of the society under which they operate. In addition, the idiosyncrasy of that family relationship plays a role. Everett (2010) from his experience of living with the *Pirahã* in *Amazon* demonstrated that all societies may not perform the motherly duties in the same way. As he illustrated, the *Pirahã* children learn to become independent once the weaning period is over. The children are treated as children only during the weaning period, after which they started to take care of themselves without the family supervision (pp. 105–107). This way of raising children is substantially different from what can be observed in many societies.

Another event described by Everett (2010) also illustrates how a social context may influence the provision of services from one person to another. In his description, a woman died by the riverbank early morning giving birth to a child. She had an urgent need for care, but nobody came to help her. This is unthinkable in some societies as in such a case, someone is sure to offer help and call for an ambulance to take the woman to the hospital. But the activity of getting an ambulance and receiving treatments from the hospital involves monetary transactions. So, in *Pirahã* society, because of the social make up, the dying women lacked that money. But in another society that money exists for the same women in a similar circumstance.

In some societies, a newborn may not be allowed to live if some pre-conditions are not fulfilled. *Jean Auell*'s provided description of an incidence of this nature in her prehistoric novel the *Clan of Cave Bear* which is the first novel of her celebrate prehistoric series *The Earth children* (Auell 1980). The novel was about a *Homo Sapiens* girl living with a *Neanderthal* group. The Neanderthal group practised the tradition of examining every newborn for any physical deformity. If any deformity is found, then the child was not regarded as fit to survive and left outside of the cave of the group for certain death by natural elements. In the novel, the Homo Sapiens girl was unwilling to accept this tradition and ensured the survival of her deformed child (deformed in the eyes of Neanderthals).

Another grim description of this nature is available in the novel *Growth of the Soil* of *Knut Hamsun* (Hamsun 1917). This novel has a much more modern setting illustrating the emergence of an industrial society from a rural background. But this novel also features infanticide by the mother as the child was born with a cleft lip, the same as her.

If these references from fiction are objected, we may look at a very modern incidence. India in the recent decades experienced a widespread occurrence of feticide. The modern inventions like ultrasonogram allow the parents to know the gender of the foetus at an early stage of pregnancy. As female children are less desired in some Indian societies, the foetuses identified as female were getting terminated. It was so widespread that the Indian government had to ban this practice by passing a law in the parliament (Imam 1994). It may be also pointed out that there also exists a business of surrogacy which is essentially renting out of the womb in exchange of money (Qadeer and John 2009). The readers may here also be referred to the literature on the disturbing incidence of filicide (Stanton and Simpson 2002).

The above examples should be sufficient to establish that our social activities involve transactions of goods and services from one person to another, but those activities are not uniform. Even, the activities caused by something biological and apparently universal like motherly love also depend on individuals and societies. However, such transactions of goods and services are always taking place and will take place making the existence of money universal. On the other hand, the type of the ability, i.e. the money may differ depending on the individual and social contexts. Some of those transactions may not be viewed as money in our traditional sense, but have the potential to turn into one, for example, the replacement of the motherly love by the care of a paid nanny. Such activities exist in every society in usual money or non-money forms, hence money as the ability to obtain goods and services from others is prevalent in every society. But not only do they vary by societies, within a society they vary by individuals. The existence of money therefore is a conditional existence that differs due to individual and societal idiosyncrasies.

Money in the form of cash or credit is not immune from this conditional existence. For example, money in the form of notes is issued by governments or relevant authorities. The existence of the government provides legitimacy of the money issued. The notes issued in a country usually has no ability to acquire goods and services in other countries. With the fall of governments, the value of those currencies collapse. So, the existence of money in the form of pounds, dollars, etc., is also relative conditional existence. They cease to be money or go through modifications once the conditions are not fulfilled. Interestingly, while notes/cash usually cease to be money in another country, money in the form of bank deposits may remain useful. In addition, when it comes to the export or import of goods, money in the form of cash, notes, etc., have very limited ability, while money as bank deposits maintains the ability. It again proves the context dependent existence of money.

We have so far proved the universality of money with reference to the examples from human biology and stated that credit and commodity theories are not adequate in explaining all human transactions. However, even without any clear biological underpinning, money nevertheless exists. Such existence is apparent in mega projects that create *public goods*. Modern public goods are financed through taxation. The ancient world has seen many mega projects even before the construction of pyramids. Graeber and Wengrow (2021) in a monumental book titled *The Dawn of Everything* attempted to reconstruct the human history and provided references of several ancient mega cities. These cities provided some type of public goods requiring the communities to come together for design, construction, and maintenance, and evidences are not pointing towards any central organising body like what is seen in ancient Egypt. This can be also said about the first city of the world known as *Çatalhöyük*, where the houses in that city shared the same walls and had entrance via doors on the roof. The formation of those cities or structures provides proof of mobilisation of resources from one person to another person with or without the existence of any centralised taxing body. Boyd and Richerson (2022) also identified large scale cooperation for public goods in small societies. Hence those societies had some mechanisms for the transfer of goods and services, though not in usual forms. In the absence of money how can one explain such mobilisation of resources? Surely money like gold coins, ingots, shells, etc., cannot explain those mobilisations as there exists no proof of commodity money in those periods. Those projects may have used some accounting techniques like the one that can be found in the *Illiad* of *Homer*. Schmandt-Besserat (1978) proposed that ancient Sumerians may have invented writing as a consequence of the use of clay tokens to keep records. In a similar fashion, Graeber (2014) discussed that the need to use something as the unit of account may have resulted in some commodities regarded as money. Therefore, those ancient mega projects may have used some unit of account, for example, gold or oxen.

However, gold and oxen cannot build Pyramids or cities or public places, instead woods, stones, and other building materials are required; and those are acquired and put into use by the human labour. The mobilisation of human labour in this manner can be only explained by some pre-existing social conditions compelling the individuals and households to spare labour for those common causes. Our identification of money as the ability to obtain goods and services from others well explains such mobilisation of resources. Ancient mega projects or existence of public goods in some societies therefore are examples of pre-existence of money in societies and supporting the claim of the universality of money; with or without the core biological instincts like the motherly love.

The Name of the Money

The naming of the section has been influenced by *Umberto Eco*'s novel *The Name of the Rose*. However, it is probably better to start referring to a famous quote from *Romeo and Juliet* of *William Shakespeare,*

> What's in a name? That which we call a rose
> By any other word would smell as sweet.
> (Shakespeare 2023, Act 2)

Shakespeare is right that the name of the rose does not change the smell of the rose. The same is about the identification of money in the book. Whatever is the name used in practice, they all must represent the fundamental characteristics of the ability to obtain goods and services from other people. Roses come in different shapes, colours, and even the smell differs time to time. But they are all roses, nonetheless.

This is often forgotten when people talk about money. Money appears in the real world in different names like dollars, pounds, etc. But the most problematic is, that money is called using different names in different contexts. This is nicely demonstrated in some YouTube videos (see YouTube 2023) which the readers will easily find by searching using terms like *"Money has different names"*. The videos state that money takes different names in different contexts such as in marriage *dowry*, in charity *donation*, when paid to the government called *tax*, when given to children called *allowances*, when obtained from banks called *loan*, when paid to schools called *tuition fees* and in courts called *fines*. But in all cases, they are nothing but money.

There is nothing wrong in using different names as they all can be true at the same time. Like a rose can be called a flower as both are true at the same time. The same goes to the different uses of money for the name they take in different contexts. This has been previously identified by the economics literature. The mingling of money with other terms like output has been clearly identified by Rossi (2001) when stating about the relationship between money and output that goods and services cannot be measured independent of money (pp. 77–79). Similarly Gowland (2000) referred to a statement that *"Money buys goods and goods buy money, but goods do not buy goods"* (pp. 9).

However, economic profession in general seems not worried about the commonality. It resulted in many misleading terms such as the often-used term called *fiat money*, which refers to a government issued money not backed by gold. They seem to forget to consider that the gold itself has no intrinsic value. The value of gold is itself dependent on the willingness of the countries and people to keep assets in gold and in the past to use that as money.

The readers also should have noted the commonality between wealth and money. The wealth refers to various assets in physical or in usual money forms. The existence of wealth can provide the owner the ability to obtain goods and services from others. Hence, money can be used as a synonym for wealth depending on the context and vice versa. A similar commonality is observed between money and capital. Capital is the resource, e.g. machineries used in production along with the labour. Capital allows the owner to obtain further goods and services hence depending on the context capital can be expressed using the term money. Which term is more suitable to use depends on the context. When someone only refers to the production process, the term capital may be more suitable or instead the term like machines, factories, inputs, etc., can be used. But the same production process allows the owner to obtain further goods and services and the ownership of capital, in that context, is synonymous to having money.

Therefore, the name of the money should not dictate the analysis and one should also be open to accept that money shares commonalities with many other things and those things in some situations can act as money and in other contexts may not. Some readers may be familiar about the story of a group of men describing an elephant. This is a well-known story which probably originated from the Indian subcontinent. I first came to know about the story from my primary school teacher. It goes like this:

> A group of blind men heard that a strange animal, called an elephant, had been brought to the town, but none of them were aware of its shape and form. Out of curiosity, they said: "We must inspect and know it by touch, of which we are capable". So, they sought it out, and when they found it they groped about it. The first person, whose hand landed on the trunk, said, "This being is like a thick snake". For another one whose hand reached its ear, it seemed like a kind of fan. As for another person, whose hand was upon its leg, said, the elephant is a pillar like a tree-trunk. The blind man who placed his hand upon its side said the elephant, "is a wall". Another who felt its tail, described it as a rope. The last felt its tusk, stating the elephant is that which is hard, smooth and like a spear. (Wikipedia 2023)

As the elephant is very big, the blind men failed to appropriately describe the elephant. The story surely wanted to provide some moral lessons, but what I found striking was that none of them were incorrect; that within their localised experience, they managed to describe the elephant correctly, making them all simultaneously correct. Money is in a similar manner so large that it encompasses all human activities, that it may become manifested in a particular form in a particular context, that is different from the manifestation of money in another context. But both still remain true. There exists a general truth about the elephant that it is ***a very large animal***. When it comes to the particular section, it is like a wall in some parts, like a tree in some, and like a snake in some other parts. Similarly, money remains everywhere and all the time as the ability to obtain goods and services from others. But in particular time and space, it takes different forms and names, based on the idiosyncrasies of those time and space.

References

Auell, J. 1980. *The Clan of Cave Bear*. New York: Crown Publisher.

Boyd, R., and P. Richerson. 2022. Large-Scale Cooperation in Small-Scale Foraging Societies. *Evolutionary Anthropology: Issues, News, and Reviews* 31 (4): 175–198.

Everett, D. 2010. *Don't Sleep, There are Snakes: Life and Language in the Amazonian Jungle*. London: Profile Books.

Friedman, M. 1968. *Dollars and Deficits: Inflation, Monetary Policy and The Balance of Payments*. Englewood Cliffs, New Jersey: Prentice-Hall. https://archive.org/details/dollarsdeficitsl00frie/page/n3/mode/2up. Accessed 9 Sep 2022.

Gowland, D. 2000. *Money, Inflation and Unemployment*. Pearson Education South Africa. https://archive.org/details/moneyinflationun0000gowl_r6a4/mode/1up. Accessed 6 Jul 2023.

Graeber, D. 2014. *Debt: The First 5000 Years*. 2nd Revised Edition. London: Melville House Publishing.

Graeber, D., and D. Wengrow. 2021. *The Dawn of Everything: A New History of Humanity*. London: Penguin Random House.

Hamsun, K. 1917. *Growth of the Soil*. Translation by W.W. Worster. Published in 2004 by Project Gutenberg. https://www.gutenberg.org/cache/epub/10984/pg10984-images.html. Accessed 8 Nov 2023.

Imam, Z. 1994. India Bans Female Feticide. *BMJ* 1994 (309): 428. https://doi.org/10.1136/bmj.309.6952.428.

Innes, M. 1913. What is Money? *The Banking Law Journal* 377–408. https://www.newmoneyhub.com/www/money/mitchell-innes/what-is-money.html. Accessed 26 Aug 2022. Reprinted at Wary (2004).

Keynes, J. 1930. *A Treatise on Money*. London: Macmillan.

Qadeer, I., and M. John. 2009. The Business and Ethics of Surrogacy. *Economic and Political Weekly* 44 (2): 10–12.

Rossi, S. 2001. Money and Inflation: A New Macroeconomic Analysis. Cheltenham: Edward Elgar. https://archive.org/details/moneyinflationne0000ross. Accessed 7 Jun 2023.

Ryan-Collins, J., T. Greenham, R. Werner, and A. Jackson. 2012. *Where Does Money Come From?* London: New Economics Foundation.

Schmandt-Besserat, D. 1978. The Earliest Precursor of Writing. *Scientific American* 238 (6): 50–59.

Shakespeare, W. 2023 *Romeo and Juliet* from The Folger Shakespeare. In *Folger Shakespeare Library*, eds. Barbara Mowat, Paul Werstine, Michael Poston, and Rebecca Niles. https://folger.edu/explore/shakespeares-works/romeo-and-juliet/. Accessed 26 Sep 2023.

Stanton, J., and A. Simpson. 2002. Filicide: A Review. *International Journal of Law and Psychiatry* 25 (1): 1–14.

Voltaire. 2014. *Candide and Other Works*. Translated by Fowler James. Ware: Wordsworth Editions.

Wary, L. 2004. *Credit and State Theories of Money*. Cheltenham: Edward Elgar Publishing.

Wikipedia. 2023. *Blind Men and An Elephant. Wikipedia: A Free Encyclopaedia*. https://en.wikipedia.org/wiki/Blind_men_and_an_elephant. Accessed 27 Sep 2023.

YouTube. 2023. YouTube Search Results Using "Money Has Different Names". https://www.youtube.com/results?search_query=money+has+different+names. Accessed 12 Sep 2023.

CHAPTER 7

Money as the Ability and Inflation

Abstract The chapter establishes the relationship between inflation with money defined as the ability to obtain goods and services from others. It starts with pointing to the fact that though inflation is regarded as a major problem; studies specific to inflation are limited, even within the discipline of economics. The chapter discusses the economic analysis of inflation, and demonstrates its insufficiency, as it only looks at aggregate price levels, and as such is not applicable to economic systems with many heterogeneous entities comprising of sectors, regions, families, and individuals. Inflation is instead a problem of distribution that impacts different segments of an economy differently through uneven changes of the money, i.e. ability. The book then discusses that the changes in the price level are better explained by the changes in the bargaining power, and thereby the balance of money, i.e. the ability of various segments of the economy. The balance is impacted by non-market issues, the stored ability, and the ability to borrow from the future. A change in the balance implies that individuals may find them requiring to utilise more of physical and mental power to create the ability to acquire goods and services. Inflation thereby is the need to utilise more body and mind to create the ability, i.e. money to acquire a wide range of goods and services.

Keywords Inflation · Quantity theory of money · Phillips curve · Demand-pull and cost-push · Non-market · Stored ability · Borrowed ability · Distribution

M. Chowdhury, *Money and Inflation*,
https://doi.org/10.1007/978-3-031-52356-4_7

The general increase in prices is known as inflation. The opposite of it is deflation or negative inflation. The use of the term inflation can refer to the economy as a whole or can be sector specific such as the inflation of consumer goods, producer goods, food items, or a specific good such as apples.

While I do not disagree with what is stated in the above paragraph, from the perspective of this book, a more comprehensive analysis of inflation is required. Specifically, the relationship between *inflation and money as the ability to obtain* needs to be established; and it is the main objective of this chapter. This chapter is organised to first look at the usual economic theories on inflation, that are guiding the policies undertaken by central bank authorities. Then the limitations of those views are identified, and the focus is directed to extend the concept of inflation and reframe in terms of human abilities. The relationship between money and inflation is established and along the way the relationship between money and price level is investigated.

Economic Analysis of Inflation

Inflation is a much-discussed topic in everyday human life. A good number of books and articles in economics addressed inflation, but it seems to have not managed to occupy the centre stage. Inflation tends to come as a by-product or a vehicle of some other important issues that economists like to focus on, for example to manage expectations of economic activities or to promote growth and investment in the economy. Inflation itself is not regarded as the biggest issue.

This treatment of inflation in economics is really surprising as inflation or rising price level is one of the most unpopular economic indicators, which usually guarantee the toppling of a government through vote or other means. Hence inflation itself is regarded as the biggest issue when comes to economic policies, and all over the world the governments would direct efforts to contain inflation. The incidence of inflation stays in the memory; such as the well-known German or Zimbabwean hyperinflations.

Within the economic literature, the relationship between money and inflation is probably best expressed using the *Quantity Theory of Money*. A textbook-level exposure to the theory is available via Gowland (**2000**), but in many books and online articles extensive coverage of the subject can be found. The theory demonstrates a relationship between money supply and the output, as such when output is fixed, the increase in the money supply results in the increase in the output. These views may have influenced four alternative definitions proposed by Bronfenbrenner and Holzman (1963), specifically in the definition of inflation is *a condition of generalized excess demand, in which "too much money chases too few goods"*. *Milton Friedman* is the most famous proponent of the quantity theory and added the statement that inflation is always and everywhere a monetary phenomenon (Friedman 1968).

One of the well-known studies on economics shows that unemployment and inflation are negatively related, that is government policies to reduce unemployment or to increase output is associated with a higher rate of inflation. This is known as *Phillips curve*, which is due to an article by *William Phillips* (Phillips 1958). The Phillips curve generally predicts a negative relationship between inflation and output. However, in the 1970s the world economy experienced higher inflation without the increase of output, commonly known as stagflation. This phenomenon is explained via the idea proposed by *Milton Friedman* where the government expansionary policies are in the long run essentially ineffective in increasing output, however, may lead to inflation (Schwarzer 2018).

Otherwise causes of inflation are attributed to two categories, One is demand-pull and another in cost-push (Rossi 2001, page 5; Schwarzer 2018). This is better explained by a diagram as done in Fig. 7.1:

The readers must note that the diagram is only an illustration. The real things are happening in the economy. The demand of the economy

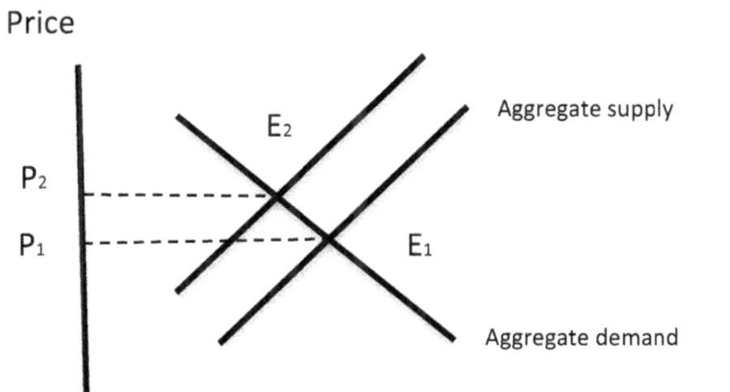

Fig. 7.1 Price level and economic models

is called aggregate demand that combines the consumption, investment, and government expenditures, i.e. the activities that demand goods and services from the economy. This is represented by a downward sloping curve/line on the price-output axis as shown in Fig. 7.1. It shows that as the price level goes up the demand of the economy does down. On the other hand, the supply of the economy is called the aggregate supply. It is illustrated by an upward sloping curve/line, which shows the supply goes up as the price goes up. The balance of the economy is reached where the demand is equal to the supply, such a situation is called the equilibrium, and in the diagram is represented by the intersection of the demand and supply lines at E1. That balance or equilibrium is reached when the price level of the economy is equal P1. It also determines the output level of the economy, which has not been explicitly shown on the diagram, but easily identifiable on the horizontal axis. Now assume a change in the supply due to some underlying cost change as such the whole supply curve shifted to the left causing the economy to supply a lower amount at the previous price level. It results in an imbalance and eventually a new balance is reached at P2, where the economy wide price is higher, i.e. instead of P1 is P2.

What is illustrated in Fig. 7.1 is an example of a cost-push inflation where the price level experiences an increase due to the change of supply. In a similar fashion there can be also a demand-pull inflation (not shown in the diagram), where the demand curve shifts to the right. This can occur, for example, when there is an increase of the expenditure of the government. When there is a recession, macroeconomic theories, known as the *Keynesian economics* would recommend for an increase in government expenditure, to take the economy out of recession. This policy is assumed to create a demand-pull inflation, but the inflation is regarded as desired in that perspective.

However, inflation is invariably everywhere an unpopular economic event, whether it helps or does not help the economy. Some economists would regard it as a tax on money (Friedman 1968), however, people generally do not view it in that way. Rather inflation is unpopular as they observe the decrease of their purchasing power. The general readers may also find all those terms like aggregate demand or supply and equilibrium puzzling. As an economist, I myself cannot make sense out of them. The economy is in fact consisting of many heterogenous entities and cannot be aggregated; hence there exists not aggregate demand or supply in the economy. Aggregation can only exist in monetary terms via the unit of account, as stated by Rossi (2001), but in real terms it cannot take place. Additionally, the economy faces regional, occupational, and family-level idiosyncrasies. But the usual measure of inflation and economic models resort to generalisation without any intention to make amends.

The generalisation is visible in the measurement of inflation by comparing some basket of goods. For example, the Office for National Statistics (ONS 2023a) in the UK collects data of about prices of 700 items. The data is used to measure the *Consumer Prices Index* (CPI), or the price of the shopping basket of typical consumers. In other countries, inflation is measured in a similar manner. Sector-level inflation can also be calculated such as the shopping basket of producers is used to calculate *Producer Price Index*.

The generalisation results in generalised economic policies. The Bank of England targets to have 2% inflation yearly to facilitate smooth planning for the future as "*if inflation is too high or it moves around a lot, it's hard for businesses to set the right prices and for people to plan their spending. But if inflation is too low, or negative, then some people may put off spending because they expect prices to fall. Although lower prices sounds like a good thing, if everybody reduced their spending then companies could fail and people might lose their jobs*" (Bank of England 2023). This view also drives the policies of other central banks.

But as we stated before, this usual measure of inflation of policies does not make much sense to the common people. For example, the media would often report of inflation rate of 5% or 10%. But the consumers view it differently. They see that the prices of what they regularly buy have gone up substantially. For example, the price of a pack of eggs has gone up from £1 to £2 in 6 months. It is common for consumers to compare the price increases with their income.

The real consequence to be considered is therefore the unfavourable movement of the prices impacting individual consumers. It is accordingly connected to the distribution of the purchasing power or the ability. Some economists previously have addressed the question of distribution (e.g. Budd and Seiders 1971), however, it is usually ignored in economic analysis. IMF (2023) though have mentioned of distribution, provided only a very light touch, lacking in details. In order to explain the issue of distribution, let us assume an economy where the income of all inhabitants in the form of dollars or pounds has gone up by 10% and without any change of the production or supply of goods and services. In this situation, inhabitants may perceive that they have now higher ability as the income has gone up. However, they are not capable of purchasing more as the availability of goods and services is unchanged. So essentially ability or purchasing power (what can be obtained) remains unchanged. As the income has gone up by 10%, the economy is likely to experience a 10% price hike without any change of the welfare. The price hike in this case is an inflation as per a generalised measure; however, the inhabitants will observe no decrease in the purchasing power in acquiring goods and services.

However, this never is the case. In real life, goods and services experience different level of changes, an example of which is given in Table 7.1. It shows the average annual growth rate of price rate of some items. All items have experienced a price increase, but the rate is higher for some items like sugar (50%), olive oil (47%), and cucumber 47%. The distribution of the price hikes and changes of income therefore should be compared. Say, in an economy, 50% experienced an income hike and the remaining 50% did not. Then again, more money on average will chase the same amount of goods and services causing a price hike. But the 50% without the increase in the income now experience a decrease in the purchasing power of the ability and are worse off.

The previous discussion shows that the unpopularity of inflation cannot be due to the general increase of the price level, rather the individuals

Table 7.1 Average prices of items and annual growth rate May 2023

Name (weight or size)	*Average price*	*Price last year*	*Annual growth (%)*
White sliced bread 750–800 g	£1.35	£1.11	22
Frozen chicken nuggets 220–600 g	£2.49	£1.91	30
Frozen breaded/battered white fish 400–550 g	£5.11	£4.04	26
Olive oil 500 ml–1 litre	£6.16	£4.19	47
Hard cheese per kg	£10.04	£7.45	35
Lemonade 2 litre	£0.94	£0.72	30
Granulated white sugar per kg	£1.10	£0.73	50
Cucumber each	£0.84	£0.57	47
Plums per kg	£2.95	£2.45	21
Cook-in sauce 350–520 g	£1.93	£1.36	41
Hot chocolate drink 250–400 g	£2.93	£2.43	21

Source ONS (2023b)

having to pay more than the previous amount of money (i.e. ability) across a wide range of goods and services. Inflation should be looked at as a problem of uneven distribution of the increase of the prices where the individuals are facing a decrease in purchasing power or in other words the ability to obtain goods and services. In order to address inflation, there is a need to look deeper into determination of prices and in the next section, we will demonstrate that price level and ability to obtain goods and services from others, i.e. money are interconnected. Evaluation of that relationship is a necessary ingredient in analysing inflation.

Money, Price Level, and Inflation

Inflation, to begin with, should be studied as a change in prices of individual goods and services, and only then implications of the general changes in the price level can be understood. Hence the determination of the price level is an important aspect of studying inflation. The usual explanation, that are widely available in text books are that prices are determined by a mechanism of demand and supply, or in order words, via the comparison of the willingness of the consumer to purchase and the willingness of the seller to sell. Often the seller and buyers have asymmetric market power, information, etc., and all those influencing factors come together in determining the market prices. To explain the determination of prices, the textbooks use diagrams of a similar nature as given in Fig. 7.1, but instead of the aggregate demand and supply, the demand and supply of individual goods like apples/oranges are considered.

However, this mechanism described is devoid of the concept of money. The prices are determined, but there is no process to describe the buying and selling of products. In real life buying and selling cannot take place without money. Figure 7.2, explains the process of buying.

Figure 7.2 describes a generalised process of buying. Physical or mental works produce goods and services. The person can then sell those goods

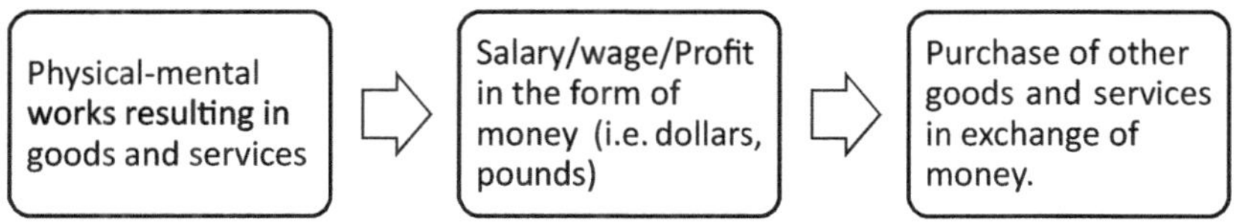

Fig. 7.2 The process of buying

and services to other people, and obtain goods and services for final or intermediate consumption or money in the form of dollars, pounds, etc. The person can also be employed by another person, hence may only receive salary/wage in the form of dollars, pounds, etc. The person then uses that money to buy other goods and services as desired. A similar figure can be made to demonstrate the process of selling of a product.

In the real-life markets, buyers and sellers compare their monetary endowment with what they can get in the exchange. They look at what they must give up in order to purchase the desired item. This demonstrates the willingness to buy and sell and it may depend on many factors including the information available on the overall demand and supply in the market.

The price of a product is what one must give up in order to obtain a product. In other words, *the ability, i.e. money needs to be spent to obtain a product is its price*. The amount one must spend/give up depends on the relative bargaining power of the parties involved a transaction (see also Chapter 4). When the price goes up, it implies that one must give up more, i.e. employ a higher amount of physical and mental work for acquiring the previous amount of goods and services. It is true that prices are always counted by using monetary units. However, we really need to think beyond simple monetary units. From the context of the book, the relevant question is not exactly the question of price, rather what is required from an individual in order to obtain, e.g. 3 apples from a supermarket. This may be a combination of ability; such as the ability to go to supermarket and the ability to spend one pound.

As in Chapter 3, assumed that the supermarket sells 3 apples for 1 pound. In order to sell 3 apples, the supermarket required a combination of ability of the individual, however, receives only one tangible reusable ability, the one pound that gets transferred from the individual to the supermarket. The supermarket therefore has an incentive to obtain the monetary endowment, i.e. the reusable ability of its customers and the reusable ability it demands is actually the highest possible amount within the specific context. For example, when a supermarket sets the exchange rate of 3 apples for one pound, it can also set 4 apples for one pound. It also has a limit of how much less it can charge. If the cost of procuring 3 apples is less than the exchange rate allowed by the context under which it operates, it will eventually not sell apples.

The role of bargaining is described in Figs. 7.3 and 7.4:

Fig. 7.3 Bargaining to buy

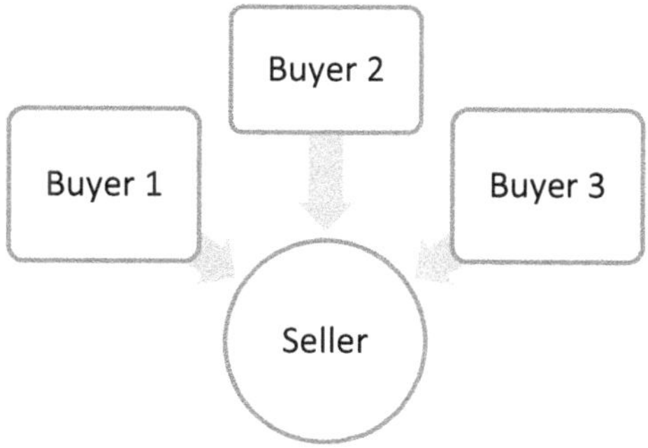

Fig. 7.4 Bargaining to sell

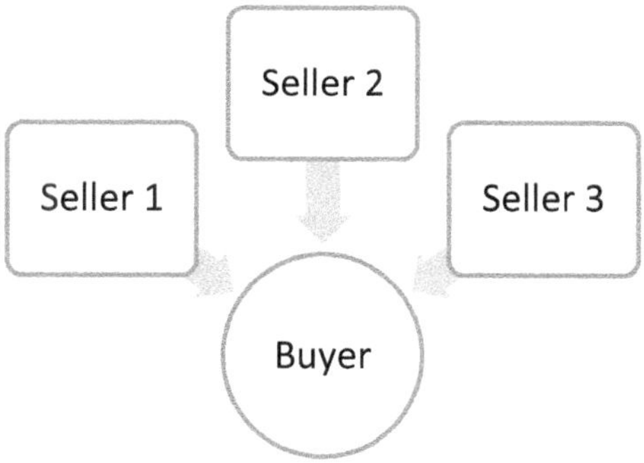

In Figs. 7.3 and 7.4, we illustrated typical bargain situation to buy and sell. In Fig. 7.3, one seller is selling the product, and 3 buyers are willing to buy the product. So, the seller in this situation is able to exercise some power over the buyers. The seller will sell the product to the highest bidder, i.e. who is willing to pay the highest price, but also will utilise the competition among the buyers to drive up the price through some mechanisms. In Fig. 7.4 the opposite has been described. There are 3 sellers, however, only 1 buyer. Hence the buyer is in a better position to seek a lower price from the sellers.

Figures 7.3 and 7.4 are simple and to some extent self-explanatory. The situation described above is significantly modified by three factors—(1) Non-market issues, (2) stored ability, and (3) borrowing from the future or borrowed ability. To understand the relationship between market and non-market issues in a transaction, let us refer to the example of the market for a nanny that was discussed in Chapter 6. We must first recognise that there exists no market for a mother's love. It is not transferable and even a mother herself can only sense the love. It is similar to a pain or pleasure, that can only be realised by the person who experienced that. However, the services performed by a mother are saleable, such as a mother can also work as a nanny. Now compare between the two situations. Firstly, a mother providing a service to a child out of love and in return obtaining motherly satisfaction, and secondly, a mother working as a nanny and providing services to a child for accessing goods and services (through usual money like dollars, pounds, or in other forms). The question of price is appliable for the second case as a mother may demand more money for a service or the service receivers (the family of the child) may demand to pay less to the mother for the services. Though there is no market for a mother's love, it provides the pre-condition for forming the market for nanny as the mother would not hire a nanny without the pre-existence of the motherly love. Therefore, the existence of the motherly love is playing a role in the existence of a market for buying and selling of the childcare service. Hence the buying and selling of taking care of a child is contingent upon the existence of motherly love (or a love of a similar nature).

However, the non-saleable factors, sometime may even prevent the formation or limit the operation of the market, i.e. buying and selling of products. This is very much true for individual or family activities but also notable at the national level. This is notable for the products that are regarded as protected by the nation states or households. This attitude is observable in the production, consumption, and trade of rice. It is well identified in the literature that only a very small fraction (e.g. 7%) of production of rice enters the global trade as rice is consumed mostly in the same country of production (Muthayya et al. 2014). Similarly, the decision of the farmers to produce rice may not be motivated by market forces; rather by the motive to ensure the food security of their households (There exists an extensive literature, see Toquero et al. 1975 as an example). Going back to our example of motherly love, a wealthy mother may just prefer to take care of the children by herself, though capable of hiring a nanny. The economic activity of this particular mother therefore is not directly observable in the market. However, the price mechanism or the process of bargaining captures the influence of these non-market factors. If a mother decides not to hire a nanny, then the available nannies of the market do not have the ability to extract goods and services from that mother. If no mother or family want their children to be taken care of by others, then the available nannies have no ability to obtain goods and services from others in exchange for the childcare service.

The previous discussion showed that the market price reflects many non-market characteristics of an economy or society. The price is like the tip of an iceberg that only shows a part of the whole thing. In addition to the non-market factors, an important component of that iceberg is the stored money or ability of an economy. The stored ability of an economy can take various forms, and depending on the form and ownership of the stored ability, the bargaining power changes. The storage of the ability is actually of prime importance when analysing matters related to price hikes. The abilities are generally not storable, such as labour power, for example, the ability of someone to perform the childcare service perishes with time and if someone does not work in a day, that work hour cannot be used on another day. However, money in dollars, pounds, gold coins, gold ingots, etc., provide the assurance and to some extent an illusion of storage. The ability may remain stored also in the form of wealth or capital. Economic disparity of an economy therefore is very much down to the difference in the stored ability of the inhabitants. All human beings are endowed with ability via the use of body and mind. So, the basic disparity in that sense is not that much, though there can be some extraordinary human beings with superhuman ability. For example, the skill of *Michelangelo* or the ability of an ingenious computer programmer. Otherwise most human beings are equal in the use of body and mind, and all skills (including extraordinary ones) perish with time. Hence those abilities can only influence market prices if they are allowed to be stored and handed over to the future users in an asymmetric manner. In determination of prices, depending on the ownership of the stored ability, the bargaining powers get modified by the perishment of some abilities on one hand and the storage of some abilities on the other hand. Those who are endowed with only labour are probably the weakest in this position of bargaining, and have the potential to be exploited. Even a line of literature on industrialisation and development has the basis in the exploitation of labour. This is represented by the well-known *Lewis model* of economic development proposed by *Arthur Lewis* (Lewis 1954). The literature suggests that many developed countries have surplus labour in the agricultural sector. This surplus labour is the stored ability of those economies, that can be unleashed for achieving the goal of economic development in a relatively inexpensive manner, i.e. to facilitate the growth of the manufacturing sector at a lower wage rate.

A last matter to be discussed is the influence of the borrowed abilities, specially from the future. It is an important component in the modern economy which has expanded through the expansion of the financial sector. The ability to borrow from the future varies from person to person and it significantly impacts the ability to acquire goods and services at present. In that sense the future incomes also chase the goods and services to be acquired at present.

The preceding discussion shows that the price level is reflective of the two parties' money, i.e. the ability to obtain from the other party, and is determined by a series of interactions with non-market issues, stored money, and borrowed money. They together contribute to the number of active as well as potential buyers and sellers of various economic activities taking place at a particular time and space. The exchange rates are hardly stable as the abilities are always changing, and from time to time may tilt in favour or against a party or the other. Hence a party in a certain situation may find the need to employ more ability to acquire the previous level of goods and services. It may happen across a wide range of goods and services and akin to inflation as understood in usual sense.

Inflation is therefore a situation where an individual, a group, or the whole economy may find themselves facing the need to increase the utilisation of ability (i.e. money) to acquire a wide range of previous level of goods and services. Inflation is related to the increase in the price level but it is only a cause of concern when human beings find themselves utilising more of their body and mind.

However, the story of inflation has more to it. The identification of inflation as the increase in the use of human ability by itself necessitating that extended explanation. Otherwise, the logical loop of the analysis is not closed, but it has also real validity as was the case of our identification of money. As inflation is the increase of the use of human abilities, we must take into consideration the increase of activities due to the increase in human desire. Hence inflation can be also self-inflicted. Surely an increase in the prices induces an individual to work more, however, the same effect is observed when the demand of an individual increases. Such an increase in the demand may also compound an existing case of inflation in addition to creating one. The causes of inflation therefore are multifaced and an analysis of that to be provided in the next section.

References

Bank of England. 2023. *Inflation and the 2% Target*. Bank of England. https://www.bankofengland.co.uk/monetary-policy/inflation. Accessed 14 Jul 2023.

Bronfenbrenner, M., and F. Holzman. 1963. Survey of Inflation Theory. *American Economic Review* 53 (4): 593–661.

Budd, E., and D. Seiders. 1971. The Impact of Inflation on the Distribution of Income and Wealth. *The American Economic Review* 61 (2): 128–138.

Friedman, M. 1968. *Dollars and Deficits: Living with America's Economic Problems*. Hoboken, NJ: Prentice-Hall. https://archive.org/details/dollarsdeficits l00frie/page/n3/mode/2up. Accessed 9 Sep 2022.

Gowland, D. 2000. *Money, Inflation and Unemployment*. Pearson Education South Africa. https://archive.org/details/moneyinflationun0000gowl_r6a4/mode/1up. Accessed 6 Jul 2023.

IMF, 2023. *Inflation: Prices on the Rise*. International Monetary Fund. https://www.imf.org/en/Publications/fandd/issues/Series/Back-to-Basics/Inflation#:~:text=Inflation%20can%20also%20distort%20purchasing,a%20pensioner's%20purchasing%20power%20falls. Accessed 17 Jul 2023.

Lewis, A. 1954. Economic Development with Unlimited Supplies of Labour. *The Manchester School* 22 (2): 139–191.

Muthayya, S., J. Sugimoto, S. Montgomery, and G. Maberly. 2014. An Overview of Global Rice Production, Supply, Trade, and Consumption. *Annals of the New York Academy of Sciences* 1324 (1): 7–14.

ONS. 2023a. *Consumer Price Inflation Basket of Goods and Services: 2023*. Office for National Statistics. https://www.ons.gov.uk/economy/inflationandpriceindices/articles/ukconsumerpriceinflationbasketofgoodsandservices/2023#:~:text=1.-,Main%20changes,Prices%20Index%20(RPI)%20baskets. Accessed 24 Aug 2023.

ONS. 2023b. *Exploring How the Average Price of Individual Items Has Changed in the Last Year*. Office for National Statistics. https://www.ons.gov.uk/economy/inflationandpriceindices/articles/exploringhowtheaveragepriceofindividualitemshaschangedinthelastyear/2023-05-03. Accessed 5 Jul 2023.

Phillips, W. 1958. The Relation between Unemployment and the Rate of Change of Money Wage Rates in the United Kingdom, 1862–1957. *Economica, 25*(100): 283–299.

Rossi, S. 2001. Money and Inflation: A New Macroeconomic Analysis. Cheltenham: Edward Elgar. https://archive.org/details/moneyinflationne0000ross. Accessed 7 Jun 2023.

Schwarzer, J.A. 2018. Retrospectives: Cost-push and Demand-pull Inflation: Milton Friedman and the "Cruel Dilemma." *Journal of Economic Perspectives* 32 (1): 95–210.

Toquero, Z., B. Duff, T. Anden-Lacsina, and Y. Hayami. 1975. Marketable Surplus Functions for a Subsistence Crop: Rice in the Philippines. *American Journal of Agricultural Economics* 57 (4): 705–709.

CHAPTER 8

The Causes of Inflation

Abstract Inflation is identified as the increased need to use the human body and mind to acquire goods and services from others. Accordingly, the human-made causes of inflation are twofold, the first one is self-inflicted caused by the increased desire to consume, and the second one is due to distortionary policies of governments that change the balance of the ability of various segments. The chapter discusses how human desires have expanded in recent times causing them to work more to fulfil those needs. Modern parenting is discussed as an example. The chapter analyses the post-Covid-19 inflation, specifically, the housing market crisis as an example of how government policies can distort the balance of an economy. Some famines have been analysed to show the impact of policies favouring one party at the expense of another one.

Keywords Human desire · Consumption · Modern parenting · Sports · Social media influencers · Poverty · Famine · Entitlement approach · Covid-19 · Bank of England · Housing market crisis

An increase in the price, as we have identified in the previous section is *the increased need to utilise human body and mind to create abilities to obtain a good or service from another person/party*. And *inflation is the occurrence of this need across a wide range of goods and services*. Inflation

M. Chowdhury, *Money and Inflation*,
https://doi.org/10.1007/978-3-031-52356-4_8

is therefore directly connected to money, which is the ability to obtain goods and services from others. The fundamental in understanding inflation is therefore the understanding of causes of the increased utilisation of human body and mind.

In an exchange both parties transact goods and services and those goods and services act as money for respective parties. The changes in the price level implies that the increase of the ability of one party which also means the decrease of the ability of another party. This can be reflected by a notion of price expressed in terms of dollars, pounds, etc. The fact is that such changes would always happen as life and human activities are not static, and one with a better bargaining power in one situation may find weakened status at another time and space. The advantage or weakness in one situation may get cancelled out by the advantage or weakness in another situation. This becomes a matter of concern when one party finds itself being disadvantaged in most of the situations, implying a general decrease in purchasing power across a broad range of goods. Such can also happen to large or various sections of the economy, instead of just a small number of people.

The balance between different forms of abilities, however, only explains a part of inflation. What if human beings by themselves decide to utilise more of the body and mind to create the ability to obtain more goods and services from others? Such a behaviour is an outcome of the expansion of the needs, and may have the same effect as the changes of the balance of abilities in increasing the utilisation of body and mind.

Therefore, the analysis of inflation needs to address two issues. One of them is the external force, beyond the immediate control of an individual, such as the increased supply of money by governments as such human beings may find themselves working more for the previous level of goods and services as a consequence of the price hike. This is well addressed at the policy level. But the other one, or the internal one, remains unaddressed at the policy level, which is the increased needs/desires of human beings for consumption, causing them to utilise more of their body and mind.

Inflation due to Increased Human Desire

It is down to the individuals to use the human body and mind to create the ability, i.e. money to obtain goods and services from other people. If human desire expands, individuals may feel the need to employ an increasing amount of human body and mind. It implies that inflation can be the consequence of our lifestyle, which may or may not get compounded by institutional policies or external shocks. In order to elaborate this point, note that human abilities are sourced by physical and intellectual human labour. What we buy and consume is ultimately down to the utilisation of the labour power. If we demand less, less is the need to utilise our human labour.

To put this into perspective let us assume a traditionally structured household; comprised of the husband, the wife, two children, and two elderly parents living in a traditional agricultural society. The husband works in the field and the wife looks after the household works. They may receive support from parents, specifically when it comes to looking after younglings; but it is mainly the works of husband and wife that provide the means for all members of the family. The dependency ratio here is 3 to 1. Now assume that the children go to a school. Then even the school also depends on the fees received from the husband and wife. Similarly, some other out of family activities may depend on the labour of husband and wife such as recreational activities or religious services. Hence all other activities in addition to the basics of life are demanding goods and services from the husband and wife of the family. The husband and wife may accordingly need to work more for the provision of all those demands. The husband and wife may feel that the time and effort are not taking them far but still desire and strive to provide all those services.

What we describe above, though hypothetical, is reflective of the modern realities. In modern time, we can observe an explosion of activities that are going beyond basic necessities of life. Moreover, these are piling up with every passing day. This is experienced by people who have the exposure to modern parenting, and it is well described by an illustration in *New York Times* (Grose 2020). It depicted some activities the parents and children perform in regular basis costing time and money. Surely schooling and providing basic education are essential in modern times, and usually state level operators take the responsibility of providing those services. However, modern parents are increasingly seen to be paying for and accompanying their children to sports, music, dance, drawing lessons etc., which can be rather categorised as voluntary.

It should be stated that most of those activities performed produce no result for the children. It may sound controversial but true. Take for example the coaching for sports. Because of the lack of open space and the general trend of not using free spaces (open fields, front gardens, etc.)

for playing games like football, cricket, etc., almost all sport activities are conducted in organised manner by clubs in designated time and space. These activities are conducted in such a manner that the children will in the future play at national or professional levels. This aim is likely to be linked with the emergence of sport for exhibition instead of enjoyment, a phenomenon well studied by *Norbert Elias* and his co-authors (Elias and Dunning 1986).

Only a very small fraction of those hopefuls can make it to the top (Gregory 2023). The parents must accompany their children to those activities and pay fees. But the space to play at the top level is very limited, and because of that, most children are unable to reach the top level irrespective of their talent and dedication. Hence these efforts get largely wasted. Ryan et al. (2016) studied the impact of organised sport activities on family financial situation. The study has found that families may invest close to 10% of the income of the family. The children have been identified to have higher parental pressure to perform as well as less enjoyment and commitment. Nevertheless, the social pressure on parents for continuing such activities is immense. In recent times, a culture of *involved fathering* and *intensive mothering* parenting ideologies have emerged for middle and upper class parents, and a parent's *moral worth* is evaluated by their children's successful participation in sport and other activities. Specifically, a new ideology for fatherhood has emerged implying that the fathers' moral worth is evaluated based on the meaningful time spent with their children (Daly 1996; Trussell and Shaw 2012).

Modern parenting is just one example, but other examples can be given, and readers are encouraged to find such from their own personal experiences. There is a need to be also a bit open minded in finding those examples. An example of this nature can be organising a lavish marriage ceremony or a birthday party that can throw a family into debt, the need of which is surely a social construction (See Bloch et al. 2004 for research on rural India). In recent times birthday parties also have become very much ritualistic (See Klein 1981; Shoham 2023).

It is not to say that those activities are not enjoyable, for example, the time the parents would spend with their children or to see the bright face of children opening the birthday gifts. It is just the opposite most of the times, however, human body and mind have limited capacity and will never be able to perform all desired roles. Hence all those roles also come with certain level of dissatisfaction and a sense of failure. Many must also take debt in order to perform those socially desired roles which in effect create guilt ridden indebted individuals (see Chowdhury 2022).

In effect, the modern time has observed an increased desire to consume. More and more items are getting added to our consumption bundles; and consequently, the need to use the human body and mind has increased causing inflation, irrespective of the increase in the price level. Think of a typical household and the electronics items the households will have at home. Only 30 years ago, a typical household would have just one car, one television, one radio, one refrigerator, and one telephone. Some might also have a dish washer and a washing machine. The same household now would also have several laptops/computers and mobile phones and additional electronic devises, but still will look to buy the latest models of all those items. The life was just fine 30 years ago as it is now. People ate, drank, enjoyed life, and died at the average age of 80. Nothing significant has changed as per the quality of life, and if any, may have only reduced. However, for some reason our preference for what we must have at our disposal has changed and our bodies and minds are working more to acquire those devices and to find time to use them. Internet browsing on Facebook, YouTube, Instagram, X (Formerly Twitter), and other platforms takes significant amount of everyday time. A huge industry has developed with people who are recognised as *social media influencers*, which did not exist 10–15 years ago. These platforms and influencers are making money through advertising, that are eventually paid off by the viewers/users. Life may have become more exciting in this age of mass decentralised communication but surely people are using more and more of their bodies and minds to create value for those service providers. Not only that we consume more, but there is also a tendency to think that the consumption flow will remain constant throughout our lives. We also expect to have the same or similar level of consumption for our family members and the responsibility of that is increasingly getting delegated to the apex bodies such as governments.

The changes and extended demands interact heavily with the development of the storage of ability in modern societies. Biologically, the ability of the human body and mind to create goods and services changes with time. At some point, human body and mind cannot perform tasks desired by others. The ability to work perishes, but in order to have a smooth consumption, the person must have access to resources. i.e. the ability to obtain goods and services from other people. Abilities in stored forms allow people to have that access, and money in the form of dollars, pounds, etc., provides that storage facility. Some assets, such as properties also allow the storage of ability. However, some goods and services cannot be stored, for example, services of a doctor cannot be stored and must be consumed at the point of creation.

Hence money in the form of dollars, pounds, etc., those coming with the storage facility is always coming in interaction with things created at present. It may appear that people have their savings, and that is used in the future for consumption. Hence at this point of time the consumption is reduced. The diagram below has been constructed to demonstrate that the reduction of consumption or expenditure is actually not the case.

Figure 8.1 describes the process. Whenever people deposit dollars, pounds, etc., into banks or financial institutions the institutions use that money, almost without any delay, for lending or making investments. Banks keep some balances, but only to the extent as needed. The remaining is quickly used for lending. Another example of savings leading to investment is the pension funds. Pension is a long-term investment, that working people would put away to cover the expense of the retired life. Hence pension implies a reduction of the current disposable income of individuals. However, the pension fund managers immediately use the money to invest in different types of financial assets (Investopedia 2022). These investments generate income for another group of people and hence lead to consumption. Therefore, all those saving activities are not reducing the current level of expenditure, instead a mechanism of transferring the money in the form of dollars, pounds, etc., from one group of people to another group of people, who would use them for immediate consumption or expenditure.

In addition, people are seen increasingly borrowing from the future. This is typically true for housing loans but also true for loans like student loans or even credit cards. These loans are extended on the promise that the households or individuals will pay back in the future. These again put pressure on the current level of consumption. ONS reported that

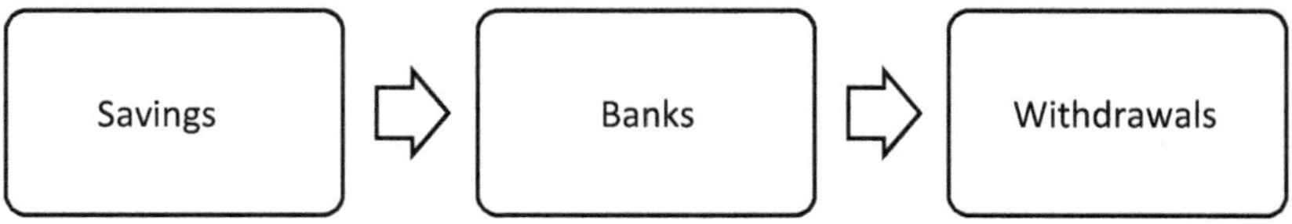

Fig. 8.1 Savings and withdrawals

the UK total household debt from 2016 to 2018 was 11% higher than the previous period of 2014 to 2016 and about 91% of household debt was property debt (ONS 2023). The property debts, as mentioned previously, are long-term debts, repayment of which are assured through future income. A similar trend is also observed in the USA where the property finances (mortgages) have the largest share (Wallace 2023).

Housing is an essential human need and taking loans for that cannot be argued against. However, many of the goods and services demanded are not human essentials or can be labelled as invented needs, and are stretching the human activities. Viewing inflation in this manner seems connected to two recent movements. One is called minimalism and the other one is called Degrowth. Minimalism is a philosophy of lifestyle recently becoming popular and has been featured in a Netflix documentary (Netflix 2021). One of the features of the philosophy of minimalism is to get rid of excess stuff, which may even include stuff with emotional values. Though it has become popular in recent times, it is not a new concept as many have also advocated minimalism in the past (Wilson and Bellezza 2022). Even one of the stories that I read in my childhood primary school advocated for minimalism. The story is about a king trying to find happiness. The doctor suggested that he would become happy if he could wear the shirt of the happiest person. The king's men started looking and finally managed to find that person. When the person was asked for the shirt, they found that the happiest person had no shirt. So, the moral of the story is that if you have no belongings, you will be the happiest.

This may seem a bit extreme, but with no doubt, it can be stated that the inflation of our demand for acquiring goods and services and how that is impacting our well-being needs to be considered. Another important movement that may be connected is called *Degrowth*. Degrowth is a planned reduction of energy and resource use designed to bring the economy back into balance with the living world. It may also imply planned reduction of the GDP of the economies of the world, particularly of the developed countries. The Third World countries may be exempt from the path of Degrowth but some would prefer to include those countries in the Degrowth movement (see Kallis et al. 2012; Hickel 2021).

The proceeding analysis shows that all those factors identified previously (see Chapter 7) seem to cause internal inflation, i.e. the non-market issues such as the desires of the individuals, the storage of the ability, and the borrowing of the ability. They form a triangle that finally results in increasing the employment of human body and mind.

Inflation due to Government Policies

In the previous section, we addressed inflation that is increased utilisation of the human body and mind due to the expansion of needs/desires for consumption. However, all will agree that in the modern world, the states and state bodies have acquired immense power in regulating human behaviour. It is true that modern corporations have created global monopolies but at the same time they often receive extensive patronisation from the states. Example of this is the collaboration between Spacex and NASA (Mann 2020). Similarly, it is often stated that many Chinese companies have received direct support from the Chinese government allowing them to prosper globally.

The analysis of inflation is not complete without looking at the role of state bodies. This is not a new view as it is well known that government policies for growth and employment may raise the price level. Central banks all over the world have various mechanisms to control inflation rates as measured via price indices. However, the inflation in our book is identified as the need for the human body and mind to work more to acquire goods and services. We therefore need to look at the impact of policies from that perspective, instead of just looking at the overall increase in the price level of the economy. The government policies change the balance of the relationship between parties and favours one over another.

This balance of relationships and how that impacts human beings are dependent on growth, decline, or stability of economic systems. In a growing system, even with a distorted distribution, all may still be better off, i.e. not have the severe negative impact of inflation. In a declining system all may become worse off, example of which is a war-time situation as experienced during World War II. Almost all countries of the world faced hardship during that time.

However, the policies taken by the ruling class may distort the distribution in favour of some groups at the expense of the others. This can happen at any time, including during a conflict. An example of the distortionary policy comes from the *Bengal famine* in the 1940s. It is to be noted that the Indian subcontinent at that time was colonised by *Great Britain*. The attention of the British colonial rule was the war against the Japanese force in the Southeast Asia, and policies were taken to support that effort, though disfavoured the people of Bengal. This matter has been extensively studied by *Amartya Sen* in a book titled *Poverty and Famines* (Sen 1981). He also studied some famines in other countries, and defined the concept of *exchange entitlement* which is closely associated with the concept of money developed in this book. In his words,

> In a market economy, a person can exchange what he owns for another collection of commodities. He can do this exchange either through trading, or through production, or through a combination of the two. The set of all the alternative bundles of commodities that he can acquire in exchange for what he owns may be called the 'exchange entitlement' of what *he owns*.. (Sen 1981, p. 4)

Amartya Sen illustrated that some great famines were caused by the loss of the entitlement to food. Specifically in the *Great Bengal famine* of 1943, which saw the death of more than 1.5 million people, the food shortage was not that significant to cause that widespread starvation. Rather, it is the loss of entitlement of some particular groups that caused the famine. He observed that the rice producers (both rich and poor) did not suffer, however, the villagers not engaged in rice production such as fishermen, craftsman were the main victims of the famines as the exchange entitlement moved against them. The role of the state-level policies causing the famine is clear in the following observations,

> This was, to a great extent, a result of general inflationary pressure in a war economy. Bengal saw military and civil construction at a totally unprecedented scale, and the war expenditures were financed to a great extent by printing notes. (p. 75)

> the prohibition of export of cereals in general and of rice in particular from each province, which had come into operation during 1942 with the consent of the government *of India, prevented the price spiral in Bengal being broken by imports from the other provinces.* (p. 77)

> an important aspect of the famine was its association with an uneven expansion in incomes and purchasing powers. Those involved in military and civil defence works, in the army, in industries and commerce stimulated by war activities, and almost the entire normal population of Calcutta covered by distribution arrangements at subsidized prices.....could exercise strong demand pressures on food, while others excluded from this expansion or

protection simply had to take the consequences of the rise in food prices. (p. 77)

Amartya Sen, in a nutshell, demonstrated that the Great Bengal famine was an outcome of the policies taken by the British government, who was ruling the Indian subcontinent at that time. Sen also studies other famines. He showed that the *Ethiopian famine* took place with no abnormal reduction in food output, and consumption of food per head at the height of the famine in 1973 was fairly normal for *Ethiopia* as a whole. The *Wollo* region specifically experienced the famine. Sen states, *"A remarkable feature of the Wollo famine is that food prices in general rose very little, and people were dying of starvation even when food was selling at prices not very different from predrought levels. The phenomenon can be understood in terms of extensive entitlement failures of various sections of the Wollo population"*(p. 111–112). In the famine of *Sahel* in around 1970 and in Bangladesh in 1974, *Sen* found little evidence to support the concept of *Food Availability Decline* (FAD), and pointed out that the entitlement approach may be more suitable explanation. He also stated, what is widely known, that the refusal to provide food aid by the USA government played a role in the price hike of food grains in Bangladesh during that time (p. 135).

The occurrence of poverty and famine is therefore an extreme form of inflation, where human beings are unable to obtain the minimum basic necessities of life. However, it is never the case that all of the population would suffer during a crisis, unless a catastrophe happens at a *Malthusian* global scale, but even then, there are winners and losers of catastrophes.

Such a catastrophe has been observed recently through the Corona Virus Pandemic (Covid-19). It started with the outbreak of a new type of a Corona Virus, named as SARS-COV-2 in Wuhan, China with high infection and mortality rates, which subsequently spread all over the world. The Covid pandemic has claimed more than 6 million lives globally. Officially 768 million people contracted the disease, but the fact is that almost all people have contracted the virus, as one would hardly find someone not mentioning to have contracted the virus or a disease of similar nature (they may be tested or not tested for the virus). The WHO declared the pandemic in January 2020. Most of the countries of the world declared lockdowns from March 2020, where the residents were not allowed to leave their homes. The schools and most workplaces were closed or moved online. International travel completely stopped.

The global trade at that time became restricted to limited items. The lockdown continued on and off for about 2 years (See WHO 2023a, 2023b, 2023c).

The Covid lockdown posed some serious challenges. The lockdown forced people to stay at home, implying many businesses and occupations had to stop operating. The Covid pandemic has seen the governments all over the world extending support to businesses, employees, and general people (IMF 2022), motivated by a fear of a general collapse of the economy, and the law and order. It may be very unpopular to say that the way the governments (and/or state bodies like central banks) responded to the Covid pandemic has caused the post-covid inflation observed all over the world. However, this opinion is also available elsewhere as given below,

> On the demand side, many countries funnelled large sums of money to households and companies during the pandemic, to ensure that they could manage lockdowns and layoffs. That increased the money supply and may have contributed to inflation. Demand for physical goods .... rose dramatically during the pandemic, because consumers had money in their pockets and couldn't spend it on restaurants or other services. No one knows for sure exactly how much these different factors contributed. But one study by economists at the New York Federal Reserve estimated that 40% of the rise in prices in 2021 was due to supply-side factors, and 60% to demand-side factors. (Frick 2022)

> First, for the past year and a half due to Covid hardly anyone was spending money. Now that the economy is back open, people are spending and traveling and, as such, there is a bottleneck with very high demand. Our system isn't set up for this high demand level, so that causes inflation in the short term. Second, with interest rates lowered to almost zero since March of 2020, these low interest rates have spurred demand in housing which is experiencing a large backlog as well as adding to inflation worries. (Carosa 2021)

> ......demand in a pandemic economy surged because of very aggressive fiscal and monetary policies in response to Covid-19. The Obama administration's stimulus package to respond to the 2008 recession was $787 billion; the pandemic stimulus packages, between the Trump and the Biden administrations, reach around $5 trillion. That huge sum of money has helped demand come back, but unfortunately the supply chain remains hampered. (McCausland 2022)

Therefore, what is to be discussed in following pages may not be entirely new, however, from the perspective of the book, we need to explain it all in terms of our definition of money and inflation with the focus on distribution of the ability. We also will assess the role of the triangle of non-market factors, storage of the ability, and borrowing of the ability in price hikes. This will be attempted with reference to policy responses during Covid lockdown periods in the UK. This discussion is a generalised discussion and, it is to be noted that a similar analysis is possible with reference to other nations of the world. The UK has been selected for the familiarity of the author with the UK policies and the general economy.

In a modern economy like that of the UK, availability of money at the individual level depends on many factors. Most notable is the wage/salary received by individuals, but government intervention can substantially influence the ability of individuals as well as businesses. The examples of such are support packages provided by the governments and/or other entities. The ability of some sections of the economy to obtain support packages from government and other entities is their money and impacts the distribution. This is very relevant in order to understand the policy responses during Covid.

Every country in the world has values, under which some activities are encouraged, and some others are not. They form a part of non-market issues influencing economic activities of a country. The support packages offered by governments are reflective of the values of the countries in addition to the economic strength of those countries. In the UK and increasingly in the globalised world, a system of belief has become or is becoming prominent, under which the importance of businesses, entrepreneurship, growth, and investment is always emphasised. It is not to say that these values are for incorrect reasons, however, I am still referring to them as value system as those are now taken for granted, instead of understanding the contexts and outcomes. Accordingly, the businesses are often extended support packages, for example, subsidies provided to reduce the cost of production, which aim to increase the ability of the businesses to supply more at a lower price. Businesses themselves are run by human beings and owners are themselves consumers. So, the support packages have a demand increasing effect. However, as businesses are owned by only a fraction of the economy and as for any policies, support packages impact the distribution of the ability to acquire goods and services from others. The same can be stated of some other values practised in the economy, such as the practice of providing social welfare. No economy or society is devoid of value systems, but our focus is how the values practised interact with government policies, and change the distribution of money causing inflation for some sections of the economy.

When extending support to businesses it is often stated that the businesses generate output and employment. If a company closes down, it implies the loss of business for that company including the supply chains to and from the company, as well as the loss of employment of the people. It is feared that if such happens on a large scale, can severely impact the economy. This was the argument expressed in bailing out the banks following the 2008 financial crisis (Moosa 2010) as if they were too large to fail. Recently one of the energy companies was bailed out seemingly motivated by a similar view (Davies 2022; Thomas 2023). This fear of collapse is making the transfer of support to the businesses possible, and is the money, i.e. providing them the ability to extract support from the rest of the economy.

It must be noted, the expectation is that this support will also help the businesses to grow, but may not be the case in reality. Assume a pub owner struggling to keep the business afloat due to a higher operational cost. The only way out for the pub is to increase the price, which is expected to drive away the customers. Supports received, such as in the form of wage subsidy or lowering of the tax or just a direct financial support, may provide a respite to the pub owner. It means that the business is saved, enabling the owner to retain or even increase the level of profit. The pub survives but the question remains of the destination of the profit if the government does not take the support back through some lump sum taxes. The profit is not necessarily going to get invested in the pub. Nor that it will increase the wage and employment in the pub. The owner will make the investment where the benefit (monetary or non-monetary) is certain or the highest. The profit from the pub may not be reinvested at all in the pub when the owner regards that as a sinking project.

What is to be considered is the extent of the distortion in the economy; caused by the policies favouring one party at the expense of another. Support provided to a pub owner is unlikely to tip the balance of the economy; not even at a local level. However, support packages provided to the banks and financial institutions, as happened after the financial crisis of 2008, tipped the balance at a global level. This happened also during the Covid pandemic as support was extended to many sections of the economy. Hutton and Keep (2023) provides an extensive report prepared for the *House of Commons* on the support received by businesses in the UK. Though the *Furlough* scheme is often discussed, which allocated £70 billion to protect millions of jobs, at the same time the businesses received much greater support under various schemes. For example, the business loan alone was at £80.37 billion. Similarly, throughout the world, support packages were extended to every direction.

What was apparently not considered was how that support would be used. Many businesses were not operational during Covid, however paid for rents, wages, and other expenditures via the ability, i.e. money acquired from the support packages. The economy as a whole had limited expenditure opportunities, but received wages, rents, fees, etc. at or close to the pre-existing level. This inevitably resulted in increased stored ability. When someone received money during the Covid lockdown periods, that money generally stayed with that person instead of getting utilised quickly. As we have mentioned that money in the form of dollars, pounds, etc. can store the ability, which is referred to as the store of value function of money. The storage is usually done in the form of bank deposits. The Covid pandemic experienced exactly that. ONS (2022c) provided a snapshot of the impact of Covid-19 on the household expenditure and savings. The statistics reveal that the household expenditure dropped, however, at the same period the households have seen an increase in the deposits in banks. This increase in deposit in banks is therefore explained by the lack of scope for expenditure. The pandemic also prevented the investment by businesses within the economy.

This stored ability, like a raised riverbed, surely has flown in many directions determined by the economic terrain. Seemingly the property market was one of the major attractors contributing to a demand-pull inflation. During the Covid period, a number of sectors of the economy experienced significant levels of growth; notably the mortgage market (Bank of England 2022). The housing market experienced a massive increase in demand caused by the need for more space (as commonly known) following lockdown. This demand was further increased following the policy of the *Stamp Duty Holiday*. The policy was initially introduced in July 2020, then extended until 30 June 2021, to boost the UK property market during the Covid-19 pandemic. This meant that buyers completing a purchase on a property for less than £500,000 before 1 July 2021 didn't have to pay stamp duty (ComparetheMarket 2021).

Therefore, the property market observed a combination of several factors. Two of them were the increased demand for space and the support package in the form of the stamp duty holiday. As expected, the result of the policy was an increase in the demand for properties and consequent increase in the prices. Any introductory microeconomic textbooks will teach that incidence of such policy depends on the elasticity of demand and supply. As the supply of houses is relatively inelastic, the gain from the subsidy has been mostly appropriated by the sellers. The sharp increase in the house price reported by ONS (2022d) surely reflects that.

These interacted with the build-up of deposits, i.e. the stored ability. In order to buy a property, most people need to borrow from the future, i.e. obtain a loan with the promise of future repayments. In the mortgage market, the availability of the loan depends on applicants' income and the deposit. Usually, the lenders will provide 4 to 5 times of the yearly income of the buyers. The rest is to be covered by the deposit. If someone has an annual income of £50,000, the maximum lending accordingly is £225,000. Hence if that person is willing to buy a property for a price of £300,000, then the deposit will have to be £75,000 (note that it is a crude estimate).

The availability of deposits therefore ensured that one of the necessary pre-conditions of a loan, i.e. to borrow from the future, is fulfilled. The lenders do not face any such financial constraints. As long as the deposit is available and the income of a borrower provides assurance of the repayment, a lender can create money just by some accounting techniques to make the purchase possible (See McLeay et al. 2014a, 2014b; Ryan-Collins et al. 2012; Werner 2014, 2016). Moreover, the higher prices impact the lenders positively as it implies a higher amount of loan and consequent interest earnings. It has been observed that the financial institutions registered a record level of profit during the pandemic (KPMG 2021). KPMG explains that the increase of the net profit is primarily due to the reduction of the operating cost, while the net interest income also played an important role.

The people, who bought properties with the deposits, lost the ability to purchase once the sale was concluded. The ability has been transferred to the sellers and the mortgage lenders. The owners now have the properties but not as money, as the properties are unable to enter into any further transactions. The new owners have the properties, but mainly for own habitation; and are not willing or able to sell to the market soon. Those who purchased for investment must also wait some years to realise the benefit. Meanwhile they must pay back loan through instalments as the borrowing from the future comes with such a sacrifice. The instalments have gone up compared to the income of the property purchasers as they had to accept a higher price by stretching themselves to be able to climb up the property ladder, while the price hike benefited mortgage lenders significantly. Note also that the average house price in December 2021 was £275,000 and the average income was £31,400 (ONS 2022b). The loan amount considering 5 times the income is about £155,000. So, the rest is provided by buyers, i.e. about £120,000. With the deposit of about one-third or half of the property, lenders are fully secured, implying that in the event of a default, the lenders are ensured to receive the money through the forced sale of the property. On the other hand, the borrowers lacking in money are struggling to meet the current expenditure, which explains the cost of living crisis faced by this group.

What we explained above is hence completely consistent with the explanation of inflation of the book that the individuals and families are getting pushed to use more of the body and mind to create the ability to acquire goods and services. We also have noted that the economic policies during Covid significantly changed the balance of the triangle in the economy. Interestingly, even before Covid, the property market experienced an increase in prices (ONS 2022d). The increased availability of loan via money creation by commercial banks played a role, but it does not explain it all. The changes in the price are significantly down to the changes in preferences, demographic changes, and supportive government policies. It may be argued that borrowing from the future for current expenditure is true at the individual level but at the macro level, many are only paying back, so in total money creation and destruction should equate with each other. It, however, depends on the population dynamics. With a growing population, the newly created ability (output of the body and mind) is likely to be more than the destroyed ability. In addition, the preference for living alone has increased all over the world including in the UK (Kotlikof and Morris 1990; ONS 2022a). ONS reported that the number of families increased by 6.5% over the decade from 2011 to 2021. At the same time, the number of people living alone has increased by 8.3%. Thereby, availability of loans coupled with the increased demand well explains the tremendous growth of the price of housing. The Covid pandemic and consequent policies may have just expediated an already existing trend.

The explanations provided in relation to the property price hike are already well known and extensively covered elsewhere (Ryan-Collins et al. 2017; Cheshire et al. 2021). It is important to recognise that we have entirely managed to explain the price hike of the property market from the perspective of money as the ability to obtain goods and services, and to show that is due to the distributional impacts of the policies. It is to be noted that Ryan-Collins et al. (2017) on a number of occasions used the term money and purchasing power together, as such is consistent with our explanation of money.

Concluding Remarks on Inflation

In the preceding sections, we have provided an analysis of the causes of inflation and specifically addressed the global cost of living crisis. The specific sector that was analysed was the housing market. Our explanation was relatively simplistic and aimed to provide some intuitive explanations. We also note that the price hike of the property market is a complex phenomenon requiring an extensive investigation, however, our analysis indicates that it must happen due to the disruption of the triangle that we discussed. We like to point out that as the price hike refers to the issue of money, unless a thorough analysis is conducted on the nature of money (i.e. the ability in money and non-money forms) in operation of those transactions, any investigation on this matter is incomplete. Future research and economic policies should aim to understand those causes.

Also, it is to be noted that only two causes of inflation have been analysed. One of which is internal, happening due to the increase in human desire. The other one is external, due to distortionary policies. The readers will note that the commercial banks, which are known to create the money in the form of dollars, pounds, etc., through lending were not addressed extensively in this analysis. The fact is that the financial institutions are also like individuals aiming to fulfil their own objectives. The financial institutions have their own desires, but the desires come from the chief executives and shareholders of those institutions. Whatever are the views expressed by the institutions, they must come from the individuals in those places. All decisions of those institutions are human decisions, unlike what Harari (2014) stated about corporations. A corporation can never make a decision. It is only the human beings behind those corporations that make decisions. These human beings are subject to the increased desires of modern times. The desire to make of profit (and consequently obtaining bonus, promotion, etc.) by extension of loans to customers and the tendency to take loans for the fulfilment of desires are two sides of a coin. All together are human induced inflation causing human beings to work more for the fulfilment of modern needs.

Finally, the issue of internality and externality of inflation should be further discussed. There exists no pure external inflation, unless caused by an event beyond human control such as an asteroid hitting the earth. All other disasters are human-made that include war and climate disasters. The question of external and internal, however, is useful to evaluate the control of individuals on ability, i.e. money-related actions. It is true that the modern governments are formed via the votes of their inhabitants, however, once a government is elected and policies are undertaken by the ruling class, the individuals have no choice but to follow those directives, whether approve or disapprove. Similarly it can be mentioned about the rules and regulations imposed by a coloniser as the colonised has no choice but to follow those directives. It is this lack of control, that is making some causes of inflation external. This is probably also the case of the inflation faced by many poor countries in post-Covid-19 world. With the increase in the price of the US dollars, these countries are struggling to find foreign currencies to meet the import demands; specifically for some necessary items like food, energy, and medicines. The domestic hardships caused by external government policies are examples of externally caused inflation, that are beyond the control of small Third World nations. On the other hand, individuals often are also steered by the society to take certain actions. It is true also in poor countries. Some social pressures can be so strong that the individuals must follow them, as if severe consequences will follow, if those actions are not taken. However, in some actions the individuals do have a certain degree of control, such as what to wear and who to follow on social media. Those actions can be classed as internal.

Whether we class those activities as internal or external, the inflation that we observe in modern life is a combination of several factors; some caused by the individuals themselves, some by the societies they sign up to and some by the national and international state-level policies. All causing the individuals to spend more time to create money using their body and mind.

References

Bank of England. 2022. *Household Credit: A Visual Summary*. Bank of England. https://www.bankofengland.co.uk/statistics/visual-summaries/household-credit. Accessed 12 Nov 2022.

Bloch, F., V. Rao, and S. Desai. 2004. Wedding Celebrations as Conspicuous Consumption: Signaling Social Status in Rural India. *Journal of Human Resources* 39 (3): 675–695.

Carosa, C. 2021. Covid or Policy: What's Causing This Inflation Surge? *Forbes*. https://www.forbes.com/sites/chriscarosa/2021/08/23/covid-or-policy-whats-causing-this-inflation-surge/. Accessed 20 Jul 2023.

Cheshire, P.C., Hilber, C., and Schöni, O. 2021. *The Pandemic and the Housing Market: A British Story*. Centre for Economic Performance, London School of Economics and Political Science. https://cep.lse.ac.uk/pubs/download/cepcovid-19-020.pdf. Accessed 1 Mar 2023.

Chowdhury, M. 2022. The Squid Game TV Series and the Economics of Debt. *Social Science Research Network*. https://ssrn.com/abstract=4154715.

ComparetheMarket. 2021. *Stamp Duty Holiday Explained*. Compare the Market. https://www.comparethemarket.com/mortgages/content/stamp-duty-holidays/. Accessed 2 Dec 2022.

Daly, K. 1996. Spending Time with Kids: Meanings of Family Time for Fathers. *Family Relations* 45: 466–476.

Davies, R. 2022. UK Government Defends Bonuses Paid to Staff of Collapsed Firm Bulb. *Guardian*. https://www.theguardian.com/business/2022/apr/25/uk-government-defends-bonuses-paid-to-staff-of-collapsed-firm-bulb-energy. Accessed 1 Nov 2022.

Elias, N., and E. Dunning. 1986. *Quest for Excitement: Sport and Leisure in the Civilizing Process*. Oxford: Basil Blackwell.

Frick, W. 2022. What Caused Inflation. *Harvard Business Review*. https://hbr.org/2022/12/what-causes-inflation#:~:text=Supply%20shocks%3A%20Inflation%20often%20happens,the%20price%20of%20energy%20increases. Accessed 20 Jul 2023.

Gregory, K. 2023. How Many Academy Players Make it Pro? Idsoccer. https://idsoccer.com/how-many-academy-players-make-it-pro/. Accessed 6 Sep 2023.

Grose, J. 2020. The Price of Modern Parenting. *New York Times*. https://www.nytimes.com/2020/02/12/parenting/price-of-parenting.html. Accessed 7 Jul 2023.

Harari, Y. 2014. *Sapiens: A Brief History of Humankind*. London: Penguin Random House, Vintage.

Hickel, J. 2021. What does Degrowth Mean? A Few Points of Clarification. *Globalizations* 18 (7): 1105–1111.

Hutton, G., and Keep, M. 2023. *Corona Virus Business Support Scheme Statistics, Research Briefing Number CBP 8938*. House of Commons Library. https://commonslibrary.parliament.uk/research-briefings/cbp-8938/.

IMF, 2022. *Policy Response to Covid*. International Monetary Firm. https://www.imf.org/en/Topics/imf-and-covid19/Policy-Responses-to-COVID-19#B. Accessed 2 Nov 2022.

Investopedia. 2022. How Do Pension Funds Work? *Investopedia*. https://www.investopedia.com/articles/investing-strategy/090916/how-do-pension-funds-work.asp. Accessed 8 Jul 2023.

Kallis, G., C. Kerschner, and J. Martinez-Alier. 2012. The Economics of Degrowth. *Ecological Economics* 84: 172–180. https://doi.org/10.1016/j.ecolecon.2012.08.017.

Klein, J. 1981. Birthday Parties: A Study of Developmental Change in American Culture. *Central Issues in Anthropology* 3 (1): 17–27.

Kotlikoff, L., and J. Morris. 1990. Why Don't the Elderly Live with Their Children? A New Look. In *Issues in the Economics of Aging*, ed. David A. Wise, 149–172. University of Chicago Press.

KPMG. 2021. *Record Profit for Banks after a Year of Covid-19*. KPMG. https://home.kpmg/nz/en/home/media/press-releases/2022/04/record-profit-for-banks-after-a-year-of-covid-19.html. Accessed 28 Oct 2022.

Mann, A. 2020. Crewed Launch Deepens Ties Between NASA and SpaceX. *Science* 368 (6493): 811–812. https://doi.org/10.1126/science.368.6493.811.

McCausland, F. 2022. NBC. What is Causing Inflation? Economists Point Fingers at Different Culprits. https://www.nbcnews.com/business/business-news/whats-causing-inflation-economists-point-fingers-different-culprits-rcna16156. Accessed 20 Jul 2021

McLeay, M., A. Radia, and R. Thomas, 2014a. Money in the Modern Economy: An Introduction. *Bank of England Quarterly Bulletin*, p. Q1. https://www.bankofengland.co.uk/quarterly-bulletin/2014/q1/money-in-the-modern-economy-an-introduction. Accessed 22 Aug 2022.

McLeay, M., A. Radia, and R. Thomas, 2014b. Money Creation in the Modern Economy. *Bank of England Quarterly Bulletin*, p. Q1. https://www.bankofengland.co.uk/-/media/boe/files/quarterly-bulletin/2014/money-creation-in-the-modern-economy.pdf. Accessed 22 Aug 2022.

Moosa, I. 2010. The Myth of Too Big to Fail. *Journal of Banking Regulation* 11: 319–333. https://doi.org/10.1057/jbr.2010.1.

Netflix. 2021. *The Minimalists: Less is Now*. Netflix. https://www.netflix.com/gb/title/81074662. Accessed 11 Jul 2023.

ONS. 2022a. *Families and Households in the UK: 2021*. Office for National Statistics. https://www.ons.gov.uk/peoplepopulationandcommunity/birthsdeathsandmarriages/families/bulletins/familiesandhouseholds/2021#:~:text=1.,decade%20from%202011%20to%202021. Accessed 27 Feb 2023.

ONS. 2022b. *Average Household Income, UK: Financial Year Ending 2021*. Office for National Statistics. https://www.ons.gov.uk/peoplepopulationandcommunity/personalandhouseholdfinances/incomeandwealth/bulletins/householddisposableincomeandinequality/financialyearending2021. Accessed 2 Nov 2022.

ONS. 2022c. Coronavirus and the Impact on UK Households and Businesses: 2021. Office for National Statistics. https://www.ons.gov.uk/economy/nationalaccounts/uksectoraccounts/articles/coronavirusandtheimpactonukhouseholdsandbusinesses/2021. Accessed 2 Nov 2022.

ONS. 2022d. *UK House Price Index, July 2022*. Office for National Statistics. https://www.ons.gov.uk/economy/inflationandpriceindices/bulletins/housepriceindex/july2022. Accessed 2 Nov 2022.

ONS. 2023. *Debt*. Office for National Statistics. https://www.ons.gov.uk/peoplepopulationandcommunity/personalandhouseholdfinances/debt. Accessed 8 Jul 2023.

Ryan D., T.E. Dorsch, M.Q. King, and K.J. Rothlisberger. 2016. The Impact of Family Financial Investment on Perceived Parent pressure and Child Enjoyment and Commitment in Organized Youth Sport. *Family Relations* 65(2): 287–299.

Ryan-Collins, J., T. Greenham, R. Werner, and A. Jackson. 2012. *Where Does Money Come From?* London: New Economics Foundation.

Ryan-Collins, J., T. Lloyd, and L. Macfarlane. 2017. *Rethinking the Economics of Land and Housing*. London: Zen Books.

Sen, A. 1981. *Poverty and Famines: An Essay on Entitlement and Deprivation*. Oxford: Oxford University Press.

Shoham, H. 2023. Deep Conventionality, or, Tracing the Meanings of Conventional Rituals. *American Behavioral Scientist* 00027642221145025.

Thomas, H. 2023. Why is this £6.5bn Bulb Blowout Still in the Dark? *Financial Times*. https://www.ft.com/content/a3ec2dd2-f443-43e2-b58b-906e42afdc3c. Accessed 27 Feb 2022.

Trussell, D.E., and S.M. Shaw. 2012. Organized Youth Sport and Parenting in Public and Private spaces. *Leisure Sciences* 34 (5): 377–394.

Wallace, A. 2023. Americans' Debt Surpasses $17 Trillion for the First Time. *CNN*. https://edition.cnn.com/2023/05/15/economy/household-debt-credit-q1/index.html. Accessed 8 Jul 2023

Werner, R. 2014. Can Banks Individually Create Money Out of Nothing? The Theories and the Empirical Evidence. *International Review of Financial Analysis* 36: 1–19.

Werner, R. 2016. A Lost Century in Economics: Three Theories of Banking and the Conclusive Evidence. *International Review of Financial Analysis* 46: 361–379.
WHO, 2023a. *WHO Coronavirus (COVID-19) Dashboard*. World Health Organization. https://covid19.who.int/. Accessed 20 Jun 2023.
WHO, 2023b. *Coronavirus Disease (COVID-19) Pandemic*. World Health Organization. https://www.who.int/europe/emergencies/situations/covid-19. Accessed 20 Jul 2023
WHO. 2023c. *True Death Toll of Covid 19*. World Health Organization. https://www.who.int/data/stories/the-true-death-toll-of-covid-19-estimating-global-excess-mortality. Accessed 20 Jul 2023.
Wilson, A.V., and S. Bellezza. 2022. Consumer Minimalism. *Journal of Consumer Research* 48 (5): 796–816.

CHAPTER 9

Some After Thoughts and the Question of Economic Policies

Abstract This chapter looks at the book from the perspective of readers. It notes that the book aimed to provide a new analysis of money and inflation, however, it is lacking in actual applications and policy guidelines. In defence, it is stated the book serves the purpose of demystifying the money, which itself has opened up the possibility of understanding various issues that the academic disciplines and policy makers have been struggling to address. The book develops a good multidisciplinary approach linking economics, sociology, and anthropology as such will support future research. When it comes to the policy, specifically to inflation, sector-level analysis should be undertaken, however, the balance of the ability should be studied to understand the causes of inflation in those sectors. Finally, the future of money in an independent AI-driven world is discussed.

Keywords Demystification of money · Cost of living crisis · Economic policies · Future of money · AI

In this last chapter of the book, what I am going to state may be best introduced with reference to *Roland Barthes'* famous essay "The Death of the Author" originally published in 1967 (Barthes 2014). What I gather from reading the essay is that *Barthes* was proposing a reader centric view

M. Chowdhury, *Money and Inflation*,
https://doi.org/10.1007/978-3-031-52356-4_9

of the text and suggested that imposing an authorship is to impose a limit on the text. Understandably, this view generated many further works. However, my reason for referring to the essay is that, when the act of writing is finished, I am no longer capable of imparting any changes to how the text is presented and read, and my role changes from an author to a reader.

Now that I have put down my thoughts in the previous chapters, my journey as the author of the text is complete. I myself have become a reader, though the very first one. As a reader, I note two important issues. The first one is, when I started this writing, the aim was to provide a new analysis of money and inflation. But what to do with that after the completion was not under explicit consideration. It is as if a new continent has been discovered but the explorer has no idea of what to do next! It can be the first question that the readers may ask—what can be done further utilising the analysis of the book, that is using what we have realised about money and inflation. Another obvious question is about making economic policies—that is what would be the policy recommendation of the book on monetary issues?

As a reader of my own writing, I identify that the book may have managed to resolve the mystery of money. The mystery is nicely expressed by some YouTube videos, which have been mentioned earlier (Chapter 6), which any reader will be able to find by searching using words like "money has different names". The videos are stating that money gets different names as per the context such as in marriage dowry, in charity donation, when paid to the government called tax, when given to children called allowances, when obtained from banks called loans, when paid to schools called tuition fees and in courts called fines (see YouTube 2023). All those names have mystified money. The book therefore may contribute to this demystification.

After the demystification, one can note that the fundamental to so-called money, whatever form it takes or whatever it is called, is the ability to obtain goods and services from others. Hence all those talks about money may only be partially revealing the truth and what needed is the understanding of the origin and continuation of the ability in different contexts. Following this realisation, the readers may find the society to become characterised by monetary relationship, i.e. the ability which keeps all together. But the ability is based on individual and social idiosyncrasies; making the socio-economic relationship fragmented and indetermined, even though in operation under a national umbrella with a single currency such as dollars or pounds.

Whatever it is called and whatever form it takes, the money remains forever in existence as the ability to obtain goods and services from others. Hence those who dreamed of a moneyless society and perceived the money to be the cause of all problems had it wrong from the beginning. Those thoughts are applicable only to the representation of money in various forms, but those forms only are in existence due to the presence of ability. Then if there is any problem with representations of money, then that background money is to be looked at, not just the forms it takes. Those who preached for a new form of society, must address money, coexisting with human beings, otherwise the construction of those Utopias remains incomplete. The previous attempts for reformation of societies may have faced the limitations of looking only at the forms.

Within the academic disciplines of economics, sociology, and others, this study of money may inform some new outlooks. The views reflected in the book from time to time appeared here and there in fragmented forms but never received the prime focus. Many previous works seemingly moved away to more traditional directions, even though sometimes made statements close to those of this book. A reader may find new ways of continuing the research taking into consideration the identification of money and inflation in this book. The discipline of sociology and economic anthropology may find the book specifically useful in extending their study of money to analyse the issue of inflation. The readers may also note the enhanced analytical capability of this book. A reviewer of the book with reference to the Austrian School stated that a slight price increase during the period of rapid productivity growth points to substantial monetary inflation that is likely to show up in asset inflation. Instead of going against this view, the book expands it! Money, according to the book, expands with the creation of new ability. The book accordingly proposes that the current level of inflation (including rising asset prices) is reflective of the overall expansion of the money. A part of the expansion is explained by the usual monetary aggregates of central banks, but the rest remains uncounted, and the book suggests to include that in the analytical framework.

All those, however, are about the future. The world at this moment is facing a cost of living crisis. The price of food and other items has gone up. Not only that, the worldwide supply chains are experiencing disruptions; many necessary items are not available. According to the analysis of the book, the readers can identify this as inflation implying individuals having to increase the employment of human body and mind to meet the demands. Though the book has identified no specific policy responses, it identifies that the principle of any government policies should be at the triangle of issues, i.e. the non-market issues, the storage of ability, and the borrowing from the future. Those to be addressed and the disruption of the balance of the three issues due to government policies to be looked at. Based on this principle, specific sector-wise policies can be undertaken.

In academic disciplines like economics, the policy-level analysis looks at the activities of national governments, but the book empowers individuals by suggesting that the individuals have some control over inflation. The detachment of individuals from unnecessary demands and the value systems may help significantly in containing inflationary pressures. This may be difficult but surely worth considering. Individuals taking some responsibility in containing inflation do not relieve the apex institutions, like national governments or central banks, of any responsibility. In apex institutions, so far, the policies aim at macroeconomic variables, but inflation actually is a problem of distribution. What therefore should to be aimed at is the removal of distortionary policies. The working tax paying people usually are impacted by distortionary policies, as such the removal of those policies should help the working people in lowering the tax burden. The role of government in managing the economy of a country to be also reevaluated. At the policy level of government, as well as businesses, it is also important to look at how the profits are distributed between various parties, especially the amount kept for reinvestment. Unnecessary investment expenditure in the name of growth can be avoided as that generates inflation by changing the balance of money in the economy without any improvement of welfare of the working people.

How about inflation caused by external factors, such as those faced by many Third World countries through the appreciation of the prices of foreign exchanges like US dollars? It may seem that in those cases the governments have no choice but to face the consequences of the changes to external environments. However, what we have stated about shielding the individuals against the domestic distortionary policies is equally applicable. Now it is the national government that needs to alter the activities in order to shield the domestic economy from adverse external changes, so that the negative consequences are minimised. These countries may rethink of their exposure to external economic factors, in a similar manner that many small nations are pointing to their exposure to climate change-related risks.

As a reader, I could at this moment think of these policies. However, a policy-level detailed analysis needs to be sector-specific and those sectors need to be looked at one by one. Additionally, the experience of countries differs as such the country-specific cases are to be looked at separately. Such studies are beyond the scope of the book. However, the basis remains the same, that is to look at the balance of the money between various fractions of the economy and how the policies would impact them. Where the policies have already created distortions, as such the housing markets, the aim of policies should be not to further aggravating the inflation. The same goes for the policy responses of a country facing distortions caused by international factors. Thereby the book also provides some policy guidelines for international economic and inflation governance in the form of avoiding distortionary policies.

The readers may wonder as even I started to wonder in writing the book that why the previous studies failed to identify money as done by the book. This is surprising given that many works had statements very close to what has been stated in the book. It includes scholars from economics, sociology, and anthropology. These scholars though made statements about money, the biggest challenge they apparently faced was to remove the influence of commodification. The previous research may also have suffered from the limitations imposed by the influence of the academic history, as such may have taken sides in a pre-emptive manner. The political views may have also influenced them significantly. This may be stated regarding two scholars who have been cited throughout this book, namely *David Graeber* and *Milton Friedman*.

The book is pointing that the reality of money and academic discussion on money are not aligned. The academic discussion has created a false (or an incomplete) world of money, which I identified has similarities with what was told by *Jorge Luis Borges* in a magnificent story titled "*Tlön, Uqbar, Orbis Tertius*" (Borges 2000). The narrator of the story came to know of an alien planet named *Tlön*, mentioned in an encyclopaedia. The encyclopaedia provided detailed description of the civilisation in that planet. Later he came to know that the planet has been imagined, and accordingly the encyclopaedia was written over centuries, by a secret society of scholars who called themselves *Orbis Tertius*. The narrator of the story then found that the imagined world of the encyclopaedia penetrated the reality, e.g. started to modify the language of the earth. The story hence is a depiction of the modification of the day-to-day reality by a constructed imagined reality. This may be the case of the academic works on money. Money, which is very much a matter of everyday life, is entirely discussed in some places without any such references or examples. And our belief of *what is money* has been modified by those academic writings and those views have penetrated everywhere; as *David Graeber* mockingly showed, that even a ghostly figure in *Madagascar* called *Kalanoro* knew of the barter theory of money (Graeber 2014, p. 28).

The readers may also pause at this time to think about the future of money. Money as defined in this book is founded on human nature. But in recent times, the advent of AI has shaken many people and there exist some worries regarding the future of mankind. I identify two issues—one is the AI becoming independent to make decisions and another is the AI being directed by human beings to make decisions. The latter already is observed in online platforms like Facebook, YouTube, etc. These platforms are known to have extensive use of AI, however, the parameter of the operation is given by human beings. This may cause some concerns as it is possible for someone to design an AI to create mass havoc. This remains a valid concern, however, the basis for such a havoc is entirely human and the underlying monetary relationship remains unchanged, so the view of the book remains applicable.

But the former takes us beyond human relationships covered in this book. If AI becomes fully independent, i.e. does not perform within human-designed parameters, then it demonstrates a clear break, and human nature is no longer a widely applicable basis for analysis. Such I regard only as a distant possibility, similar to what has been shared by *Noam Chomsky* in a recent TV interview (Chomsky 2023). Completely independent AI is like a black box; there is no reason to presume that such a non-biological entity will follow the natural rules of a biological entity. However, the general perception of AI is entirely based on human nature as seen in the movie *Terminator*. Why would an AI fight for self-preservation and start a war or kill others provoked or unprovoked? A fully intelligent and independent AI may see no need for self-preservation. Thereby presupposing the characteristics of biological beings to a non-biological AI is grossly false. We cannot say anything about the nature of money in an independent AI dominated society, as we do not even know whether such an AI will see the need to engage in transactions.

Therefore, the book remains a contemporary discussion of money and inflation based on the existence of human beings and how they transact goods and services with each other. It remains close to *Georg Simmel*'s statement that "*money is only a claim upon society*" (Simmel 2004, p. 176), though the term claim has been replaced with ability and the book does not see money in commodity form only. The future works may want to understand the evolution of that ability and the forms it took in some historical junctures. A related question is to address the distribution of ability in those junctures, and which distribution can be regarded as fair or acceptable. There can be many other associated normative questions that the readers may like to pursue. Some will be difficult, uncomfortable questions to raise, and may face moral and political challenges; but such are unavoidable, and require a comprehensive unbiased investigation, if one wants to address the complex economics of money and inflation of the twenty-first century. As the author and the first reader of this book, I presume that this book made a step forward to that goal.

References

Barthes, R. 2014. The Death of the Author. In *Readings in the Theory of Religion*, eds. E. Scott and M. Waggoner, 141–145. Oxford: Routledge.

Borges, J. 2000. Tlön, Uqbar, Orbis Tertius. In *Labyrinths: Selected Stories and Other Writings of Jorge Luis Borges*, eds. D. Yates and J. Irby, 27–43. London: Penguin Books.

Chomsky, N. 2023. Piers Morgan vs. Noam Chomsky | The Full Interview. *Piers Morgan Uncensored*. Talk TV. https://www.youtube.com/watch?v=TQ-Crh3rdQA. Accessed 28 Jul 2023.

Graeber, D. 2014. *Debt: The First 5000 Years*. 2nd Revised Edition. London: Melville House Publishing.

Simmel, G. 2004. *The Philosophy of Money*. Translated by Tom Bottomore and David Frisby from a first draft by Kaethe Mengelberg. London: Routledge.

YouTube. 2023. YouTube Search Results Using "Money Has Different Names". https://www.youtube.com/results?search_query=money+has+different+names. Accessed 12 Sep 2023.

References

AMNH. 2023. *DNA: Comparing Humans and Chimps*. American Museum of Natural History. https://www.amnh.org/exhibitions/permanent/human-origins/understanding-our-past/dna-comparing-humans-and-chimps#:~:text=But%20for%20a%20clear%20understanding,98.8%20percent%20of%20their%20DNA. Accessed 25 Jun 2023.

Aristotle. 1908. Aristotle's *Politics*. Translated by Benjamin Jowett. Oxford: Clarendon Press. https://archive.org/details/aristotlespoliti00arisuoft/page/42/mode/2up?view=theater. Accessed 8 Feb 2023.

Auell, J. 1980. *The Clan of Cave Bear*. New York: Crown Publisher.

Bank of England. 2022. *Household Credit: A Visual Summary*. Bank of England. https://www.bankofengland.co.uk/statistics/visual-summaries/household-credit. Accessed 12 Nov 2022.

Bank of England. 2023. *Inflation and the 2% Target*. Bank of England. https://www.bankofengland.co.uk/monetary-policy/inflation. Accessed 14 Jul 2023.

Bank of South Sudan. 2023. *The Bank of South Sudan*. Bank of South Sudan. https://boss.gov.ss/who-we-are/. Accessed 5 Jun 2023.

Barthes, R. 2014. The Death of the Author. In *Readings in the Theory of Religion*, eds. E. Scott and M. Waggoner, 141–145. Oxford: Routledge.

Bloch, F., V. Rao, and S. Desai. 2004. Wedding Celebrations as Conspicuous Consumption: Signaling Social Status in Rural India. *Journal of Human Resources* 39 (3): 675–695.

Bordo, M. 2007. *A Brief History of Central Banks*. Federal Reserve Bank of Cleveland. https://www.clevelandfed.org/en/publications/economic-commentary/2007/ec-20071201-a-brief-history-of-central-banks. Accessed 8 Aug 2023.

M. Chowdhury, *Money and Inflation*,
https://doi.org/10.1007/978-3-031-52356-4

Borges, J. 2000. Tlön, Uqbar, Orbis Tertius. In *Labyrinths: Selected Stories and Other Writings of Jorge Luis Borges*, eds. D. Yates and J. Irby, 27–43. London: Penguin Books.

Boyd, R., and P. Richerson. 2022. Large-Scale Cooperation in Small-Scale Foraging Societies. *Evolutionary Anthropology: Issues, News, and Reviews* 31 (4): 175–198.

Bronfenbrenner, M., and F. Holzman. 1963. Survey of Inflation Theory. *American Economic Review* 53 (4): 593–661.

Brown, D. 2018. Shoot them for What? How Muhammad Ali Won his Greatest Fight. *The Washington Post*. https://www.washingtonpost.com/news/retropolis/wp/2018/06/15/shoot-them-for-what-how-muhammad-ali-won-his-greatest-fight/. Accessed 26 Jun 2023.

Barzel, Y. 1977. An Economic Analysis of Slavery. *The Journal of Law and Economics* 20(1): 87–110. Reprinted in *Readings in Microeconomics*, Published in 2006. Edited by Khalil F. and R. Rashid. Dhaka: University Press Limited.

Britannica. 2023a. Objectivism. *Encyclopaedia Britannica*. Available on Objectivism | Ayn Rand's Ideas & Impact | Britannica. Accessed 26 Jun 2023.

Britannica. 2023b. *Gulag, Labour Camps, Soviet Union. Encyclopaedia Britannica*. https://www.britannica.com/place/Gulag. Accessed 24 Feb 2023.

Britannica. 2023c. The Normans (1066–1154). *Encyclopaedia Britannica*. https://www.britannica.com/place/United-Kingdom/The-Normans-1066-1154. Accessed 26 Jun 2023.

Budd, E., and D. Seiders. 1971. The Impact of Inflation on the Distribution of Income and Wealth. *The American Economic Review* 61 (2): 128–138.

Carosa, C. 2021. Covid or Policy: What's Causing This Inflation Surge? *Forbes*. https://www.forbes.com/sites/chriscarosa/2021/08/23/covid-or-policy-whats-causing-this-inflation-surge/. Accessed 20 Jul 2023.

Choi, C. 2017. Fossil Reveals What Last Common Ancestor of Humans and Apes Looked Like. *Scientific American*. https://www.scientificamerican.com/article/fossil-reveals-what-last-common-ancestor-of-humans-and-apes-looked-liked/. Accessed 25 Jun 2023.

Chomsky, N. 2023. Piers Morgan vs. Noam Chomsky | The Full Interview. *Piers Morgan Uncensored*. Talk TV. https://www.youtube.com/watch?v=TQ-Crh3rdQA. Accessed 28 Jul 2023.

Cheshire, P.C., Hilber, C., and Schöni, O. 2021. *The Pandemic and the Housing Market: A British Story*. Centre for Economic Performance, London School of Economics and Political Science. https://cep.lse.ac.uk/pubs/download/cepcovid-19-020.pdf. Accessed 1 Mar 2023.

Chowdhury, M. 2022. The Squid Game TV Series and the Economics of Debt. *Social Science Research Network*. https://ssrn.com/abstract=4154715.

Chowdhury, M. 2023. On Money and Inflation. *Social Science Research Network*. https://papers.ssrn.com/sol3/papers.cfm?abstract_id=4406437.

Christophers, B. 2011. Follow the Thing: Money. *Environment and Planning d: Society and Space* 29 (6): 1068–1084.

ComparetheMarket. 2021. *Stamp Duty Holiday Explained*. Compare the Market. https://www.comparethemarket.com/mortgages/content/stamp-duty-holidays/. Accessed 2 Dec 2022.

Cook, I. 2004. Follow the Thing: Papaya. *Antipode* 36 (4): 642–664.

Coomer, J., and T. Gstraunthaler. 2011. The Hyperinflation in Zimbabwe. *Quarterly Journal of Austrian Economics* 14 (3): 311–346.

Daly, K. 1996. Spending Time with Kids: Meanings of Family Time for Fathers. *Family Relations* 45: 466–476.

Davies, G. 2002. *History of Money: From Ancient Times to Present Day*. Cardiff: University of Wales Press.

Davies, R. 2022. UK Government Defends Bonuses Paid to Staff of Collapsed Firm Bulb. *Guardian*. https://www.theguardian.com/business/2022/apr/25/uk-government-defends-bonuses-paid-to-staff-of-collapsed-firm-bulb-energy. Accessed 1 Nov 2022.

Defoe, D. 2007. *Robinson Crusoe*. Oxford World's Classics. Oxford: Oxford University Press.

Denyer, N. 2014. *The Development of Dialectic from Plato to Aristotle: Review*. Notre Dame Philosophical Reviews, University of Notre Dame. https://ndpr.nd.edu/reviews/the-development-of-dialectic-from-plato-to-aristotle/. Accessed 15 Jun 2023.

Disney+. 2022. *Origin of the Journey of Humankind*. https://www.disneyplus.com/en-gb/series/origins-the-journey-of-humankind/4tGBS4pdG6tD. Accessed 27 Oct 2022.

Discovery. 2023. Big Cats. *Discovery Network International*. https://www.discoveryuk.com/category/nature/big-cats/. Accessed 25 Jun 2023.

Dodd, N. 2014. *The Social Life of Money*. Princeton, New Jersey: Princeton University Press.

Elias, N., and E. Dunning. 1986. *Quest for Excitement: Sport and Leisure in the Civilizing Process*. Oxford: Basil Blackwell.

Everett, D. 2010. *Don't Sleep, There are Snakes: Life and Language in the Amazonian Jungle*. London: Profile Books.

Everett, D. 2018. *How Language Began: The Story of Humanity's Greatest Invention*. London: Profile Books.

Ferguson, N. 2008. *The Ascent of Money: A Financial History of the World*. London: The Penguin Books.

Fisher, I. 1911. *The Purchasing Power of Money*. https://archive.org/details/in.ernet.dli.2015.264286/page/n527/mode/2up. Accessed 7 Jul 2023.

Frick, W. 2022. What Caused Inflation. *Harvard Business Review*. https://hbr.org/2022/12/what-causes-inflation#:~:text=Supply%20shocks%3A%20Inflation%20often%20happens,the%20price%20of%20energy%20increases. Accessed 20 Jul 2023.

Friedman, M. 1968. *DDollars and Deficits: Inflation, Monetary Policy and the Balance of Payments*. Englewood Cliffs, New Jersey: Prentice-Hall. https://archive.org/details/dollarsdeficitsl00frie/page/n3/mode/2up. Accessed 9 Sep 2022.

Friedman, M. 1991. *The Island of Stone Money*. Hoover Institution. https://miltonfriedman.hoover.org/internal/media/dispatcher/215061/full. Accessed 25 Nov 2022.

Friedman, M. 2016. *Milton Friedman Speaks: Money and Inflation (B1230)—Full Video*. Free to Choose Network. https://www.youtube.com/watch?v=B_nGEj8wIP0. Accessed 6 Jul 2023.

FSU. 2019. *Exporting the Exotic: Mummy Brown*. Department of Art History, Florida State University. https://arthistory.fsu.edu/ottoman12/. Accessed 9 Aug 2023.

Furness, W. 1910. *The Island of Stone Money, Uap of the Carolines*. Philadelphia: J. B. Lippincott Company. https://archive.org/details/islandofstonemon009573mbp/page/n7/mode/2up. Accessed 8 Jan 2023.

Galbraith, J. 1975. *Money: Whence It Came, Where It Went*. Houghton Mifflin Company Boston. https://archive.org/details/moneywhenceitcam0000galb_i7z8/mode/2up?view=theater.. Accessed 27 Oct 2022.

Gordon, D. 1959. What was the Labour Theory of Value? *American Economic Review* 49 (2): 462–472.

Gowland, D. 2000. *Money, Inflation and Unemployment*. Pearson Education South Africa. https://archive.org/details/moneyinflationun0000gowl_r6a4/mode/1up. Accessed 6 Jul 2023.

Graeber, D. 2014. *Debt: The First 5000 Years*. 2nd Revised Edition. London: Melville House Publishing.

Graeber, D., and D. Wengrow. 2021. *The Dawn of Everything: A New History of Humanity*. London: Penguin Random House.

Graham, A. 2022. Central Banks Drove Inflation by Printing Money, Says Former Bank Boss King. Independent. https://www.independent.co.uk/business/central-banks-drove-inflation-by-printing-money-says-former-bank-boss-king-b2083627.html. Accessed 27 Jun 2023.

Gregory, K. 2023. How Many Academy Players Make it Pro? Idsoccer. https://idsoccer.com/how-many-academy-players-make-it-pro/. Accessed 6 Sep 2023.

Grève, S. 2015. The Importance of Understanding Each Other in Philosophy. *Philosophy* 90 (2): 213–239.

Grierson, P. 1978. The Origins of Money. *Research on Economic Anthropology* 1: 1–35.
Grose, J. 2020. The Price of Modern Parenting. *New York Times*. https://www.nytimes.com/2020/02/12/parenting/price-of-parenting.html. Accessed 7 Jul 2023.
Hamsun, K. 1917. *Growth of the Soil*. Translation by W.W. Worster. Published in 2004 by Project Gutenberg. https://www.gutenberg.org/cache/epub/10984/pg10984-images.html. Accessed 8 Nov 2023.
Harari, Y. 2014. *Sapiens: A Brief History of Humankind*. London: Penguin Random House, Vintage.
Hart, K. 2022. *Self in the World: Connecting Life's Extremes*. Oxford: Berghahn Books.
Heijdra, B. 2009. *Foundations of Modern Macroeconomics*, 2nd Edition. Oxford: Oxford University Press.
Hickel, J. 2021. What does Degrowth Mean? A Few Points of Clarification. *Globalizations* 18 (7): 1105–1111.
Homer. 1997. *The Iliad*. Translated by Robert Fagles. The Softback Preview. Bath. First Published in 1990 by Viking Penguin.
Hughes-McLure, S. 2022. Follow the Money. *Environment and Planning A: Economy and Space* 54 (7): 1299–1322.
Hutton, G., and Keep, M. 2023. *Corona Virus Business Support Scheme Statistics, Research Briefing Number CBP 8938*. House of Commons Library. https://commonslibrary.parliament.uk/research-briefings/cbp-8938/.
Imam, Z. 1994. India Bans Female Feticide. *BMJ* 1994 (309): 428. https://doi.org/10.1136/bmj.309.6952.428.
IMDb. 2022. *Internet Movie Database*. Names and links of cited movies are in the article. https://www.imdb.com/. Date accessed, various date July–October 2022.
IMF, 2022. *Policy Response to Covid*. International Monetary Firm. https://www.imf.org/en/Topics/imf-and-covid19/Policy-Responses-to-COVID-19#B. Accessed 2 Nov 2022.
IMF, 2023. *Inflation: Prices on the Rise*. International Monetary Fund. https://www.imf.org/en/Publications/fandd/issues/Series/Back-to-Basics/Inflation#:~:text=Inflation%20can%20also%20distort%20purchasing,a%20pensioner's%20purchasing%20power%20falls. Accessed 17 Jul 2023.
Innes, A. Mitchell. 1913. What is Money? *The Banking Law Journal* 377–408. https://www.newmoneyhub.com/www/money/mitchell-innes/what-is-money.html. Accessed 26 Aug 2022. Reprinted at Wary (2004).
Innes, A. Mitchell. 1914. The Credit Theory of Money? *The Banking Law Journal* 31: 151–168. https://www.newmoneyhub.com/www/money/mitchell-innes/the-credit-theory-of-money.html. Accessed 26 Aug 2022. Reprinted at Wary (2004).

Investopedia. 2022. How Do Pension Funds Work? *Investopedia*. https://www.investopedia.com/articles/investing-strategy/090916/how-do-pension-funds-work.asp. Accessed 8 Jul 2023.

Kallis, G., C. Kerschner, and J. Martinez-Alier. 2012. The Economics of Degrowth. *Ecological Economics* 84: 172–180. https://doi.org/10.1016/j.ecolecon.2012.08.017.

Keynes, J. 1915. The Island of Stone Money. *Economic Journal* 25 (98): 281–283.

Keynes, J. 1930. *A Treatise on Money*. London: Macmillan.

Klein, J. 1981. Birthday Parties: A Study of Developmental Change in American Culture. *Central Issues in Anthropology* 3 (1): 17–27.

KPMG. 2021. *Record Profit for Banks after a Year of Covid-19*. KPMG. https://home.kpmg/nz/en/home/media/press-releases/2022/04/record-profit-for-banks-after-a-year-of-covid-19.html. Accessed 28 Oct 2022.

Knapp, G. 1924. *The State Theory of Money*. London: Macmillan.

Kotlikoff, L., and J. Morris. 1990. Why Don't the Elderly Live with Their Children? A New Look. In *Issues in the Economics of Aging*, ed. David A. Wise, 149–172. University of Chicago Press.

Kuroda, A. 2020. *A Global History of Money*. London: Routledge.

Lerner, A. 1947. Money as a Creature of the State. *American Economic Review* 37 (2): 312–317.

Lewis, A. 1954. Economic Development with Unlimited Supplies of Labour. *The Manchester School* 22 (2): 139–191.

Luu, C. 2016. Why We Love to Learn Klingon: The Art of Constructed Languages. *Jstor Daily*. https://daily.jstor.org/why-we-love-klingon-art-of-constructed-languages/. Accessed 21 Sep 2023.

Luxton, M. 1997. The UN, Women, and Household Labour: Measuring and Valuing Unpaid Work. *Women's Studies International Forum* 20 (3): 431–439.

Mann, A. 2020. Crewed Launch Deepens Ties Between NASA and SpaceX. *Science* 368 (6493): 811–812. https://doi.org/10.1126/science.368.6493.811.

Marshall, A., and D.W. O'Neill. 2018. The Bristol Pound: A Tool for Localisation? *Ecological Economics* 146: 273–281.

Martin, F. 2013. *Money: The Unauthorised Biography*. London: The Bodley Head.

Marx, K. 2013. *Capital*. Ware, Hertfordshire: Wordsworth Editions.

Maschler, M., E. Solan, and S. Zamir. 2013. *Game Theory*. Cambridge: Cambridge University Press.

McCausland, F. 2022. NBC. What is Causing Inflation? Economists Point Fingers at Different Culprits. https://www.nbcnews.com/business/business-news/whats-causing-inflation-economists-point-fingers-different-culprits-rcna16156. Accessed 20 Jul 2021

McNally, D. 2020. *Blood and Money: War, Slavery, Finance, and Empire*. Chicago: Haymarket Books.

McLeay, M., A. Radia, and R. Thomas, 2014a. Money in the Modern Economy: An Introduction. *Bank of England Quarterly Bulletin*, p. Q1. https://www.bankofengland.co.uk/quarterly-bulletin/2014/q1/money-in-the-modern-economy-an-introduction. Accessed 22 Aug 2022.

McLeay, M., A. Radia, and R. Thomas, 2014b. Money Creation in the Modern Economy. *Bank of England Quarterly Bulletin*, p. Q1. https://www.bankofengland.co.uk/-/media/boe/files/quarterly-bulletin/2014/money-creation-in-the-modern-economy.pdf. Accessed 22 Aug 2022.

Meikle, S. 1994. Aristotle on Money. *Phronesis* 39 (1): 26–44.

Menger, K. 2009. *On the Origin of Money*. Auburn, Alabama: Ludwig von Mises Institute.

Mishkin, F. 2009. *The Economics of Money, Banking and Financial Markets*, 9th Edition. Boston: Pearson.

Moosa, I. 2010. The Myth of Too Big to Fail. *Journal of Banking Regulation* 11: 319–333. https://doi.org/10.1057/jbr.2010.1.

Murry, H. 1844. *The Travels of Macro Polo*. Edinburgh: Oliver and Boyd.

Muthayya, S., J. Sugimoto, S. Montgomery, and G. Maberly. 2014. An Overview of Global Rice Production, Supply, Trade, and Consumption. *Annals of the New York Academy of Sciences* 1324 (1): 7–14.

Netflix. 2021. *The Minimalists: Less is Now*. Netflix. https://www.netflix.com/gb/title/81074662. Accessed 11 Jul 2023.

ONS. 2022a. *Families and Households in the UK: 2021*. Office for National Statistics. https://www.ons.gov.uk/peoplepopulationandcommunity/birthsdeathsandmarriages/families/bulletins/familiesandhouseholds/2021#:~:text=1.,decade%20from%202011%20to%202021. Accessed 27 Feb 2023.

ONS. 2022b. *Average Household Income, UK: Financial Year Ending 2021*. Office for National Statistics. https://www.ons.gov.uk/peoplepopulationandcommunity/personalandhouseholdfinances/incomeandwealth/bulletins/householddisposableincomeandinequality/financialyearending2021. Accessed 2 Nov 2022.

ONS. 2022c. Coronavirus and the Impact on UK Households and Businesses: 2021. Office for National Statistics. https://www.ons.gov.uk/economy/nationalaccounts/uksectoraccounts/articles/coronavirusandtheimpactonukhouseholdsandbusinesses/2021. Accessed 2 Nov 2022.

ONS. 2022d. *UK House Price Index, July 2022*. Office for National Statistics. https://www.ons.gov.uk/economy/inflationandpriceindices/bulletins/housepriceindex/july2022. Accessed 2 Nov 2022.

ONS. 2023a. *Consumer Price Inflation Basket of Goods and Services: 2023*. Office for National Statistics. https://www.ons.gov.uk/economy/inflationandpriceindices/articles/ukconsumerpriceinflationbasketofgoodsandservices/2023#:~:text=1.-,Main%20changes,Prices%20Index%20(RPI)%20baskets. Accessed 24 Aug 2023.

ONS. 2023b. *Exploring How the Average Price of Individual Items Has Changed in the Last Year*. Office for National Statistics. https://www.ons.gov.uk/economy/inflationandpriceindices/articles/exploringhowtheaveragepriceofindividualitemshaschangedinthelastyear/2023-05-03. Accessed 5 Jul 2023.

ONS. 2023c. *Debt*. Office for National Statistics. https://www.ons.gov.uk/peoplepopulationandcommunity/personalandhouseholdfinances/debt. Accessed 8 Jul 2023.

Phillips, W. 1958. The Relation between Unemployment and the Rate of Change of Money Wage Rates in the United Kingdom, 1862–1957. *Economica*, *25*(100): 283–299.

Plato, 1973. *Republic*. Translated by Francis Cornford. London: Oxford University Press.

Plato, 2002. *Five Dialogues*. Translated by G. Grube and Revised by J. Cooper. Indianapolis: Hackett Publishing Company.

Qadeer, I., and M. John. 2009. The Business and Ethics of Surrogacy. *Economic and Political Weekly* 44 (2): 10–12.

Radford, R.A. 1945. The Economic Organisation of a POW Camp. *Economica* 12(48): 189–201. Reprinted in Readings in Microeconomics. Published in 2006. Edited by Fahad, K. and R. Salim. Dhaka: University Press Limited.

Robinson, J. 1933. The Theory of Money and the Analysis of Output. *The Review of Economic Studies* 1 (1): 22–26.

Rossi, S. 2001. Money and Inflation: A New Macroeconomic Analysis. Cheltenham: Edward Elgar. https://archive.org/details/moneyinflationne0000ross. Accessed 7 Jun 2023.

Ryan, D., T.E. Dorsch, M.Q. King, and K.J. Rothlisberger. 2016. The Impact of Family Financial Investment on Perceived Parent pressure and Child Enjoyment and Commitment in Organized Youth Sport. *Family Relations* 65(2): 287–299.

Ryan-Collins, J., T. Greenham, R. Werner, and A. Jackson. 2012. *Where Does Money Come From?* London: New Economics Foundation.

Ryan-Collins, J., T. Lloyd, and L. Macfarlane. 2017. *Rethinking the Economics of Land and Housing*. London: Zen Books.

Schmandt-Besserat, D. 1978. The Earliest Precursor of Writing. *Scientific American* 238 (6): 50–59.

Schumpeter, J.A. 1987. *History of Economic Analysis*. London: Routledge.

Schwarzer, J.A. 2018. Retrospectives: Cost-push and Demand-pull Inflation: Milton Friedman and the "Cruel Dilemma." *Journal of Economic Perspectives* 32 (1): 95–210.

Sen, A. 1981. *Poverty and Famines: An Essay on Entitlement and Deprivation.* Oxford: Oxford University Press.

Shakespeare, W. 2023 *Romeo and Juliet* from The Folger Shakespeare. In *Folger Shakespeare Library*, Library, edited by Barbara M., P. Werstine, M. Poston, and R. Niles. https://folger.edu/explore/shakespeares-works/romeo-and-juliet/. Accessed 26 Sep 2023.

Shoham, H. 2023. Deep Conventionality, or, Tracing the Meanings of Conventional Rituals. *American Behavioral Scientist* 00027642221145025.

Simmel, G. 2004. *The Philosophy of Money*. Translated by Tom Bottomore and David Frisby from a first draft by Kaethe Mengelberg. London: Routledge.

Smith, A. 1937. *An Inquiry into the Nature and Causes of the Wealth of Nations*. New York: The Modern Library. https://archive.org/details/in.ernet.dli.2015.207956/page/n7/mode/2up

Stanford. 2023. Philosophy of Money and Finance. Stanford Encyclopedia of Philosophy. https://plato.stanford.edu/entries/money-finance/. Accessed 23 Oct 2023.

Stanton, J., and A. Simpson. 2002. Filicide: A Review. *International Journal of Law and Psychiatry* 25 (1): 1–14.

Thomas, H. 2023. Why is this £6.5bn Bulb Blowout Still in the Dark? *Financial Times*. https://www.ft.com/content/a3ec2dd2-f443-43e2-b58b-906e42afdc3c. Accessed 27 Feb 2022.

Toquero, Z., B. Duff, T. Anden-Lacsina, and Y. Hayami. 1975. Marketable Surplus Functions for a Subsistence Crop: Rice in the Philippines. *American Journal of Agricultural Economics* 57 (4): 705–709.

Trainer, T. 2021. What does Degrowth Mean? Some Comments on Jason Hickel's 'A Few Points of Clarification.' *Globalizations* 18 (7): 1112–1116.

Trussell, D.E., and S.M. Shaw. 2012. Organized Youth Sport and Parenting in Public and Private spaces. *Leisure Sciences* 34 (5): 377–394.

Uffizi, 1987. *The Uffizi: All the Gallery Room by Room*. Florence: Editrice.

Voltaire. 2014. *Candide and Other Works*. Translated by Fowler James. Ware: Wordsworth Editions.

Von Misses, L. 1953. *The Theory of Money and Credit*. New Haven, Connecticut: Yale University Press.

Wallace, A. 2023. Americans' Debt Surpasses $17 Trillion for the First Time. *CNN*. https://edition.cnn.com/2023/05/15/economy/household-debt-credit-q1/index.html. Accessed 8 Jul 2023

Wary, L. 2004. *Credit and State Theories of Money*. Cheltenham: Edward Elgar Publishing.

Wary, L. 2014. From the State Theory of Money to Modern Money Theory: An Alternative to Economic Orthodoxy. *Levy Economics Institute of bard College, Working Papers Series.*

Wary, L. 2018. *Modern Money Theory for Beginners.* Recorded Lecture, 26 April, 2018. St. Francis College YouTube Channel. https://www.youtube.com/watch?v=E5JTn7GS4oA. Accessed 20 Jun 2023.

Wengert, T.J. 2015. Martin Luther's Preaching an Indulgence in January 1517. *Lutheran Quarterly* 29: 62–75.

Werner, R. 2014. Can Banks Individually Create Money Out of Nothing? The Theories and the Empirical Evidence. *International Review of Financial Analysis* 36: 1–19.

Werner, R. 2016. A Lost Century in Economics: Three Theories of Banking and the Conclusive Evidence. *International Review of Financial Analysis* 46: 361–379.

WHO, 2023a. *WHO Coronavirus (COVID-19) Dashboard.* World Health Organization. https://covid19.who.int/. Accessed 20 Jun 2023.

WHO, 2023b. *Coronavirus Disease (COVID-19) Pandemic.* World Health Organization. https://www.who.int/europe/emergencies/situations/covid-19. Accessed 20 Jul 2023

WHO. 2023c. *True Death Toll of Covid 19.* World Health Organization. https://www.who.int/data/stories/the-true-death-toll-of-covid-19-estimating-global-excess-mortality. Accessed 20 Jul 2023.

Wikipedia. 2023. *Blind Men and An Elephant. Wikipedia: A Free Encyclopaedia.* https://en.wikipedia.org/wiki/Blind_men_and_an_elephant. Accessed 27 Sep 2023.

Wilson, A.V., and S. Bellezza. 2022. Consumer Minimalism. *Journal of Consumer Research* 48 (5): 796–816.

Wittgenstein, L. 1958. *Philosophical Investigations.* Translated by G. Anscombe. Oxford: Basil Blackwell.

World Bank. 2023. *The World Bank in South Sudan: Overview.* The World Bank. https://www.worldbank.org/en/country/southsudan/overview. Accessed 5 Jun 2023.

YouTube. 2023. YouTube Search Results Using "Money Has Different Names". https://www.youtube.com/results?search_query=money+has+different+names. Accessed 12 Sep 2023.

Zelizer, V. 1989. The Social Meaning of Money: "Special Monies." *American Journal of Sociology* 95 (2): 342–377.

Index

M. Chowdhury, *Money and Inflation*,
https://doi.org/10.1007/978-3-031-52356-4

www.ingramcontent.com/pod-product-compliance
Ingram Content Group UK Ltd.
Pitfield, Milton Keynes, MK11 3LW, UK
UKHW020258051026
15470UKWH00021B/1392
* 9 7 8 3 0 3 1 5 2 3 5 5 7 *